Kaplan Publishing are constantly finding new ways to make a difference to your studies and our exciting online resources really do offer something different to students looking for exam success.

This book comes with free MyKaplan online resources so that you can study anytime, anywhere. **This free online resource is not sold separately and is included in the price of the book.**

Having purchased this book, you have access to the following online study materials:

CONTENT	AAT	
	Text	Kit
Electronic version of the book	✓	✓
Progress tests with instant answers	✓	
Mock assessments online	✓	✓
Material updates	✓	✓

How to access your online resources

Kaplan Financial students will already have a MyKaplan account and these extra resources will be available to you online. You do not need to register again, as this process was completed when you enrolled. If you are having problems accessing online materials, please ask your course administrator.

If you are not studying with Kaplan and did not purchase your book via a Kaplan website, to unlock your extra online resources please go to www.mykaplan.co.uk/addabook (even if you have set up an account and registered books previously). You will then need to enter the ISBN number (on the title page and back cover) and the unique pass key number contained in the scratch panel below to gain access. You will also be required to enter additional information during this process to set up or confirm your account details.

If you purchased through Kaplan Flexible Learning or via the Kaplan Publishing website you will automatically receive an e-mail invitation to MyKaplan. Please register your details using this email to gain access to your content. If you do not receive the e-mail or book content, please contact Kaplan Publishing.

Your Code and Information

This code can only be used once for the registration of one book online. This registration and your online content will expire when the final sittings for the examinations covered by this book have taken place. Please allow one hour from the time you submit your book details for us to process your request.

Please scratch the film to access your MyKaplan code.

Please be aware that this code is case-sensitive and you will need to include the dashes within the passcode, but not when entering the ISBN. For further technical support, please visit www.MyKaplan.co.uk

D0362940

KAPLAN
PUBLISHING

USING ACCOUNTING SOFTWARE

(Sage 50)

STUDY TEXT

Qualifications and Credit Framework

AQ2016

This Study Text supports study for the following AAT qualifications:

AAT Foundation Certificate in Accounting – Level 2

AAT Foundation Diploma in Accounting and Business – Level 2

AAT Foundation Certificate in Bookkeeping – Level 2

AAT Foundation Award in Accounting Software – Level 2

AAT Level 2 Award in Accounting Skills to Run Your Business

AAT Foundation Certificate in Accounting at SCQF Level 5

British Library Cataloguing-in-Publication Data

A catalogue record for this book is available from the British Library.

Published by
Kaplan Publishing UK
Unit 2, The Business Centre
Molly Millars Lane
Wokingham
Berkshire
RG41 2QZ

ISBN: 978-1-78415-798-2

Printed and bound in Great Britain

We are grateful to Sage (UK) Limited for their support in the preparation of this Text.

CONTENTS

STUDY TEXT

INTRODUCTION

HOW TO USE THESE MATERIALS

These Kaplan Publishing learning materials have been carefully designed to make your learning experience as easy as possible and to give you the best chance of success in your AAT assessments.

They contain a number of features to help you in the study process.

The sections on the Unit Guide, the Assessment and Study Skills should be read before you commence your studies.

They are designed to familiarise you with the nature and content of the assessment and to give you tips on how best to approach your studies.

STUDY TEXT

This study text has been specially prepared for the AQ2016 qualification introduced in September 2016.

It uses a case study approach to guide you through the syllabus and builds up your knowledge and skills chapter by chapter. The text is based upon Sage 50 Professional and is also suitable for Sage Instant and other similar software packages.

Quality and accuracy are of the utmost importance to us so if you spot an error in any of our products, please send an email to mykaplanreporting@kaplan.com with full details, or follow the link to the feedback form in MyKaplan.

Our Quality Co-ordinator will work with our technical team to verify the error and take action to ensure it is corrected in future editions.

UNIT GUIDE

INTRODUCTION

This unit provides students with the knowledge and skills needed to carry out typical bookkeeping transactions and tasks using accounting software. In the modern business environment, processing data and information into accounting software is a necessary task in most finance roles. This unit teaches students the practical steps for processing accounting information electronically and will allow students to reinforce their understanding of the sequence in which bookkeeping tasks are carried out.

On completion of this unit, students will have the practical ability to enter accounting transactions into accounting software and to perform bank reconciliations accurately. Students will be able to enter information into accounting software and understand the main features of accounting software. They will learn how to set up general ledger accounts for new and existing businesses and process the typical bookkeeping entries expected of students at this level, including the processing of sales and purchase documentation, recording bank and cash entries and carrying out bank reconciliations accurately. Students will also learn how to produce reports using the software and understand the purpose of these reports.

Students must have access to a suitable specialised accounting software package as part of their study for this unit and for the assessment. Spreadsheet software alone will not allow full unit content coverage, so cannot be used for the study or assessment of this unit. The program selected by learning providers must be capable of producing reports in at least one of the following formats at various stages of the process: XLS, XLSX, CSV, DOC, DOCX, PDF, BMP, GIF, JPEG, PNG.

Screenshots may also be submitted using one of these formats. Assessment evidence submitted in alternative file formats will not be marked.

Using Accounting Software is a **mandatory** unit in this qualification.

Learning objectives

On completion of these units the learner will be able to:

- Set up accounting software
- Process sales and purchases transactions
- Process bank and cash transactions
- Perform period end routine tasks
- Produce reports

Scope of content

The specific items contained within each learning outcome and where to find them in this study text are detailed below.

Chapter

Set up accounting software

1.1 Enter information relating to organisation at the beginning of an accounting period   7

- set up and amend the general ledger accounts
- enter the relevant opening balance information

1.2 Set up customer accounts   6

- create customer accounts
- enter the relevant opening balance information

1.3 Set up supplier accounts   5

- create supplier accounts
- enter the relevant opening balance information

KAPLAN PUBLISHING

		Chapter
5.2	**Produce routine reports from the general ledger**	4, 8, 9, 10, 11

- produce a trial balance and audit trail
- identify additional general ledger reports required
- produce reports that meet business requirements

Delivering this unit

Unit name	Content links	Suggested order of delivery
Bookkeeping Transactions	Manual bookkeeping skills are useful underpinning knowledge for Using Accounting Software.	It is recommended that Bookkeeping Transactions is delivered either before or at the same time as this unit.
Bookkeeping Controls	Control account reconciliations and basic journal adjustments offer useful underpinning knowledge for Using Accounting Software.	It is recommended that Bookkeeping Controls is delivered either before or at the same time as this unit.

THE ASSESSMENT

Test specification for this unit assessment

Assessment type	Marking type	Duration of exam
Computer based unit assessment	Human marked	2 hours

Learning outcomes		Weighting
1	Set up accounting software	25%
2	Process sales and purchases transactions	35%
3	Process bank and cash transactions	20%
4	Perform period end routine tasks	15%
5	Produce reports	5%
Total		**100%**

STUDY SKILLS

Preparing to study

Devise a study plan

Determine which times of the week you will study.

Split these times into sessions of at least one hour for study of new material. Any shorter periods could be used for revision or practice.

Put the times you plan to study onto a study plan for the weeks from now until the assessment and set yourself targets for each period of study – in your sessions make sure you cover the whole course, activities and the associated questions in the workbook at the back of the manual.

If you are studying more than one unit at a time, try to vary your subjects as this can help to keep you interested and see subjects as part of wider knowledge.

When working through your course, compare your progress with your plan and, if necessary, re-plan your work (perhaps including extra sessions) or, if you are ahead, do some extra revision/practice questions.

Effective studying

Active reading

You are not expected to learn the text by rote, rather, you must understand what you are reading and be able to use it to pass the assessment and develop good practice.

A good technique is to use SQ3Rs – Survey, Question, Read, Recall, Review:

1   **Survey the chapter**

    Look at the headings and read the introduction, knowledge, skills and content, so as to get an overview of what the chapter deals with.

2   **Question**

    Whilst undertaking the survey ask yourself the questions you hope the chapter will answer for you.

KAPLAN PUBLISHING

3   Read

Read through the chapter thoroughly working through the activities and, at the end, making sure that you can meet the learning objectives highlighted on the first page.

4   Recall

At the end of each section and at the end of the chapter, try to recall the main ideas of the section/chapter without referring to the text. This is best done after a short break of a couple of minutes after the reading stage.

5   Review

Check that your recall notes are correct.

You may also find it helpful to re-read the chapter to try and see the topic(s) it deals with as a whole.

Note taking

Taking notes is a useful way of learning, but do not simply copy out the text.

The notes must:

- be in your own words

- be concise

- cover the key points

- well organised

- be modified as you study further chapters in this text or in related ones.

Trying to summarise a chapter without referring to the text can be a useful way of determining which areas you know and which you don't.

Three ways of taking notes

1   Summarise the key points of a chapter

2   Make linear notes

A list of headings, subdivided with sub-headings listing the key points.

If you use linear notes, you can use different colours to highlight key points and keep topic areas together.

Use plenty of space to make your notes easy to use.

3 Try a diagrammatic form

The most common of which is a mind map.

To make a mind map, put the main heading in the centre of the paper and put a circle around it.

Draw lines radiating from this to the main sub-headings which again have circles around them.

Continue the process from the sub-headings to sub-sub-headings.

Annotating the text

You may find it useful to underline or highlight key points in your study text – but do be selective.

You may also wish to make notes in the margins.

Revision phase

Kaplan has produced material specifically designed for your final assessment preparation for this unit.

Further guidance on how to approach the final stage of your studies is given in these materials.

Further reading

In addition to this text, you should also read the 'Accounting Technician' magazine every month to keep abreast of any guidance from the examiners.

An introduction to computerised accounting

1

Introduction

The aim of this manual is to guide you through the computerised accounting aspects of your studies.

To complete this manual you will need an understanding of the basics of double entry bookkeeping and a copy of SAGE which is an integrated computerised software package for accounts. There are a number of versions of this manual uses **Sage 50 Accounts version 18.** This version of Sage is very similar to Sage Instant Accounts version 17 and therefore you should still be able to use this Text for Sage Instant, as well as many other accounting software packages, without too much difficulty, although you may find that some of the screen-shots will differ.

Kaplan Publishing also produce a separate Study Text for Sage One software, which is an online service and as such has functionality not covered in this Study Text. Please check to ensure you have the correct study materials for your course and if using Sage One for your assessment, you are strongly advised to purchase the Using Accounting Software Study Text dedicated to Sage One (ISBN 978-1-78415-623-7).

The manual uses a **case study approach** to guide you step-by-step. It assumes that you have never used a computerised accounting package before. Even if you have, it is worth starting at the beginning to ensure that you don't 'jump ahead' too quickly.

You will find assessment criteria detailed at the start of every chapter which are applicable to its content. These are taken from the learning outcomes for this particular unit.

ASSESSMENT CRITERIA
An introduction to using accounting software.

CONTENTS

1   Manual and computerised bookkeeping

2   Benefits of a computerised system

3   Accounting documents

4   Coding

5   Risks of using a computerised system

1 Manual and computerised bookkeeping

The double entry system of bookkeeping that is still used today was developed in Italy in the fifteenth century. With the introduction of affordable and reliable information technology in the last thirty years, it was perhaps inevitable that business organisations would look to find ways to computerise their bookkeeping systems. Now it is rare to find an organisation which does not use some form of computer to aid in the day-to-day record keeping that is an essential aspect to running a business, whether large or small.

For very small organisations, a simple spreadsheet to record monies in and out of the business may suffice. However, once a business becomes larger or more complex, it may be beneficial to introduce a computerised bookkeeping system. There are many proprietary versions on the market, each of which works in a similar way. However, they will each offer different approaches to data entry, presentation of reports and so on, as well as different 'extras' such as stock management modules, budgeting and tax planning. Some systems also allow a company to integrate a computerised payroll function.

2 Benefits of a computerised system

The main benefits ascribed to a computerised bookkeeping system are:

- Quicker, more efficient processing of data
- Fewer mathematical errors – because the system completes all the double entry and other mathematical functions (e.g. calculation of percentages) there is reduced opportunity for human error.
- Accounting documents (e.g. invoices, statements etc) can be generated automatically, using tailored documents designed to incorporate company details, logos etc.
- The range of information that can be easily produced in reports is wide and varied, meaning businesses can report to various internal and external groups (e.g. management, directors, shareholders, banks etc) in an appropriate format.
- There is no need for manual processing of data – computerised bookkeeping systems complete all the double entry automatically.

- Hardware and software prices have fallen dramatically over the last thirty years, making a computerised system affordable to all organisations.

- Allow data to be easily transferred into other programs – e.g. a spreadsheet or word processing package.

3 Accounting documents

Business organisations rely on relevant documentation to record the transactions that it undertakes. Without an appropriate piece of supporting documentation, there is no way of knowing what has been bought, from whom and for how much, nor indeed what has been sold. With a high proportion of modern transactions being on credit, an accurate and comprehensive system of recording transactions is essential.

Many business documents are referred to as '**Primary Records**'. They include:

- purchase orders
- delivery notes
- purchase invoices
- credit notes
- sales invoices.

These documents are used to record business transactions in the first instance. For example, if an organisation wishes to purchase a new computer printer, it may first raise a **purchase order** which is sent to the supplier. The supplier would issue or deliver the printer along with a **delivery note**, to record the safe receipt of the goods. A **supplier invoice** requiring payment would follow. If the printer was faulty, it could be returned and a **credit note** issued.

In order for a transaction to be correctly recorded in a computerised accounting system, the appropriate documentation must first be raised and then the details entered into 'the system'; indeed, many organisations employ accounting staff whose job is primarily to enter the data accurately and completely from the source documents.

There are many other documents which are also essential in maintaining an up-to-date and accurate accounting system. Bank statements, schedules of direct debits/standing orders, supplier statements, correspondence from suppliers and customers and so on also provide invaluable information which can be used to check the computerised bookkeeping system for accuracy.

In the course of the case study which follows, you will be required to enter details from a range of source documents, and use other documents, to maintain a computerised bookkeeping system for a small company.

4 Coding

All computerised bookkeeping systems work by the use of codes. Each supplier and each customer must be given a unique code by which the computer software can recognise them. It is vital that there can be no confusion between two suppliers with similar names. For example, you may be fully aware that John Green and John Greenwood are entirely different people, but it could be easy for a computer to mix them up. Each must therefore be given a unique code by which they can be identified.

Similarly, each product manufactured or sold by an organisation may be given a unique code. Also, employees are usually 'coded' – you could check your pay slip to find your own Employee Reference Number.

Finally, every type of income or expense, asset or liability, is given a unique code to identify it. This makes entering transactions quite straightforward, since you need only refer to the relevant four digit code rather than a long narrative description.

Codes must be unique. However, they should also be recognisable by the person dealing with the system. For example, if a supplier was coded "SMITH006", this would be far more recognisable than a purely numeric code such as "0827329".

Care must be taken to issue codes that are not ambiguous. The use of a combination of letters and numbers (an alphanumeric code) often achieves this.

In SAGE, when you create a new customer or supplier record, the program will automatically suggest a code for that supplier. It does this by taking the first eight characters of the name. The suggested code for a customer called Greenwood would therefore be "GREENWOO". You may decide this is not the most appropriate code (think what the problem might be if you had two different suppliers called Greenwood), in which case you can easily change it. Many organisations have a set structure for coding, and if this is the case in your organisation you should follow it.

5 Risks of using a computerised system

Computerised accounting systems may offer a lot of advantages to businesses, but organisations must also be aware of the potential risks posed by such systems.

These risks can be categorised as:

- **Physical risks** – caused by system failure, theft, damage or loss or corruption of data, and access to systems or data by unauthorised users.
- **Virus threats** – the risk of a computer virus (or similar) being introduced to a network, with the resultant loss of or damage to data.
- **Legal threats** – from contravention of legislation such as the Data Protection Act (1998) by an organisation in the way that it stores or uses personal data.

Accounting data is particularly at risk, because it is highly confidential and potentially highly valuable to other people. Hence you must remain especially vigilant to risks to data security.

Virus threats

All computers that are linked to 'the outside world' (e.g. via a network or to the internet) are susceptible to security threats. Many people are familiar with the threat posed by viruses or other similar threats.

A virus is a piece of software that is used to maliciously infect your computer. What is more, it then has the ability to replicate itself and infect any other computer that is connected to yours. Of course, this also means that your computer is at risk of being infected by other computers as well.

Introduction of the virus to a system usually takes place when you open a file that has been deliberately infected – for example, an email attachment or a web-site, an infected piece of software, or an infected memory device (e.g. a memory stick).

The consequences of being infected by a virus are many:

- Infecting all other computers you are linked to.
- Deleting particular files – especially files which are essential to the normal operation of your computer.
- Altering files so they are no longer legible.

- Slowing down your computer by taking up huge amounts of memory – leaving your computer extremely slow and unable to perform basic tasks.

- Access your data and send it to other people.

- 'Read' your passwords for essential sites such as on-line banking – enabling somebody else to access your bank account.

- Wiping your hard-drive – essentially deleting everything from the computer.

Safeguards against viruses

Firewalls: these are designed to prevent 'hackers' gaining access to a computer network via the phone line. These can be a piece of software (now often built in to operating systems such as Windows) or a hardware firewall, which is essentially a box which acts as a barrier between the modem (the phone line into your computer) and the computer itself. An effective firewall is an essential aspect of computer safeguarding, particularly where users have access to the internet.

Effective IT policies: most organisations now have clearly defined IT policies regarding the private use of the internet and e-mails, not allowing employees to install their own software (e.g. games) on work computers.

Using virus protection software: this is the most important method of protecting computer systems. It acts as a guard dog, constantly watching for suspicious files, blocking or destroying them and advising the user that there has been an attempt to compromise the security of the system. As virus protection programs are constantly being updated with details of new viruses, it is essential that it is kept updated and current at all times. An out-of-date program is no protection against the most recent viruses.

Personal vigilance: Be very wary if you receive unsolicited emails from addresses that you do not recognise. Do not open any emails that you are suspicious of – you should report these to your IT manager or your supervisor. However, you should also be wary of emails (particularly those with attachments) from addresses you **do** recognise – remember, if somebody you know has a computer which has been infected there is a high probability that the computer will then try and attack your computer as well.

Be very careful when accessing the internet. Only use sites you need for work. Be wary of links to other sites that you do not recognise. Again, if you are in any doubt, or suspect that your computer may have been the victim of a virus, inform your supervisor.

Passwords

Passwords are one of the most common – and most abused – forms of computer security. In most businesses the access to each computer is protected by a password, as well as access to different pieces of software.

Even individual files and documents can and should be protected if they contain confidential or sensitive information.

The choice of password is very important; you should be able to remember it, but it should not be easily guessed by others. Ideally, a password should:

- Be at least 6–8 characters long
- Contain a mixture of upper and lower case letters and numbers
- Not be a recognisable word

Under no circumstances should you choose something like your own name, you child's name or your pet dog's name – these are far too easy for someone with only a small amount of knowledge about you to guess. You should also avoid obvious combinations such as 'password' or '123456'.

You should be able to remember your own password. Do not be tempted to write it down in your diary, on a scrap of paper in your top drawer, or even on a sticky note and attach it to the monitor!

You should also never tell anybody else your password – even your most trusted colleague. If you do suspect that somebody knows what your password is, you should change it immediately.

Many systems are configured to require you to change your password every few weeks – even if yours is not, this is good practice.

Backups

Occasionally data is lost, whether through an unforeseen circumstance such as a fire or through computer failure. It is therefore essential that organisation's take appropriate steps to minimise the risk of data loss, and to minimise the impact of data loss if it does happen.

Backups should be taken on a regular basis, and at least once a day in most businesses. In addition, individual files should regularly be backed up whilst working on them. There is little more frustrating than spending an hour producing a document or a spreadsheet only to lose it and not to have a back up.

Many programs (including Microsoft Office applications) have an auto-recovery function – essentially a back up is taken automatically every few minutes without the user having to do anything. If there is an interruption or failure (e.g. a power cut) only a small amount of work would be lost, and the affected file can very quickly and easily be recovered.

Copies of backups should be kept securely to prevent unauthorised access or accidental damage. It is good practice to keep a back up at a secondary location (i.e. off site). This way, if there is a fire or a burglary the backup data will not be destroyed or stolen. Some businesses may still take physical backups off site (such as a CD), but this increases the risk of that back up being lost or stolen while away from the office. It is becoming increasingly common for organisations to pay an IT company to keep remote backups electronically.

There are no relevant 'learning outcomes' applicable to backups, as these do not form part of the assessment process for AQ2016. However, you are recommended to fully familiarise yourself with how to perform backups of your accounting data.

Installing Sage for the first time

2

CONTENTS

There are no relevant 'learning outcomes' applicable to this section of the Study Text, as you will not be required to install Sage as part of the AAT assessment. Therefore, this particular chapter is designed to assist you with the initial installation process that will enable you to start using 'Sage 50 Accounts Professional' for the first time as part of your Using Accounting Software studies.

1 Installing Sage

Although you will not be required to install Sage as part of the assessment, it is important to understand the initial installation process.

When you load Sage v18 for the first time you should see the following screen:

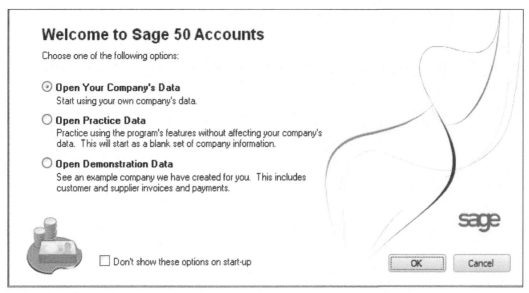

Welcome to Sage 50 Accounts

Choose one of the following options:

⦿ **Open Your Company's Data**
Start using your own company's data.

○ **Open Practice Data**
Practice using the program's features without affecting your company's data. This will start as a blank set of company information.

○ **Open Demonstration Data**
See an example company we have created for you. This includes customer and supplier invoices and payments.

☐ Don't show these options on start-up   OK   Cancel

sage

Assuming you are entering a new company (as you will be doing here, make sure that the "set up a new company data" is marked. Don't worry at this stage about the other options – just press the [Next] button.

You should now see this screen:

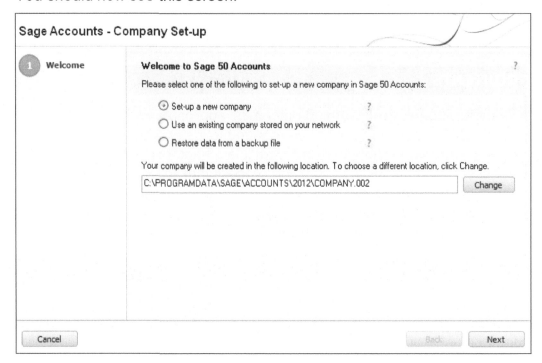

Your choice here depends on whether you are setting up a new company, or uploading existing data.

For now, you will be starting with a completely new company, so click on the "**SET UP A NEW COMPANY**" button as shown.

Once you have company details set up and saved in SAGE, it will default to that company each time you start up. However, it is easy to return to this point if you wish to enter a new company.

Setting up your company

CONTENTS

1 Case Study – background to the company

2 Setting up the company

As with the previous chapter, there are no 'learning outcomes' associated with this chapter.

During the AAT Using Accounting Software assessment, you will be required to enter information to match the details of the company given in the scenario within the real assessment. This will include the name and address of the company and also the details of their financial year.

1 Case Study – background to the company

You will be given a case study throughout this Study Text which will form the basis for activities for you to practice on Sage. It relates to a fictitious company called **TotalPhoto Ltd**. By completing the activities and entering the relevant transactions, you will learn how to do lots of tasks that are available on Sage. You will also help prepare for the AAT UACS computer based assessment as part of your AAT studies.

Background to TotalPhoto Ltd

TotalPhoto Ltd is a small company based in the market town of Miltonby, in Lancashire. It is owned by two directors, Matt Evans and Stuart Lincoln. It was established in 2004 when both Matt and Stuart left Art College. They specialise in contemporary family photography, most of which takes place in their rented studio on a small industrial estate on the outskirts of town. In addition, they also undertake a varied and increasing range of contracted photography, including weddings, dance shows, football competitions etc.

TotalPhoto Ltd has four members of staff, excluding yourself. In addition to Matt and Stuart, there is Sarala, a part-time photographer, and Michelle, the administrator for the company.

Since its inception, the company has used a manual bookkeeping system. However, the company has grown significantly in this time and Matt and Stuart now require more timely financial information on which to manage the company. They have therefore decided to implement a computerised system and to employ you as a part-time bookkeeper for the business.

We will use 30th September 2016 as '**today's date**' which is the last day of the company's financial year.

2 Setting up the company

Introduction

When you start using Sage for your case study company, you must firstly enter some information about the company itself. This is important because it will identify this particular company and appear on various reports. In addition, at this stage, you must enter the dates of the company's financial year. This is vitally important, as Sage will use this information in producing your annual accounts.

Data

You will need the following information for this session.

Company Name:	TotalPhoto Ltd
Company Address:	Unit 63
	Bailey Industrial Estate
	Fornby Road
	Miltonby
	Lancashire
	LD37 7QZ
Telephone:	01949 969 378
Fax:	01949 969 379
E-mail:	info@totalphotoltd.webnet.uk
Website:	www.totalphotoltd.co.uk
Company Reg. Number:	734928107
VAT Number:	376 096 823
Accounting Period:	1st October 2015 – 30th September 2016

Now we can begin entering the data for our company, TotalPhoto Ltd.

Activity

Enter the information onto the computerised system using the information provided in the previous box. Guidance follows.

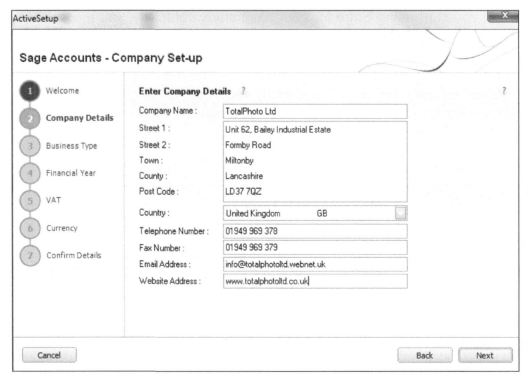

Be sure to check for accuracy – but don't worry if you make a mistake because you can always amend it later (we will look at how you can amend errors in a later chapter). Once you are happy with your entries click on the [Next] button.

Step one – Selecting the business type

On this screen you can choose a business type for your business, this amends the nominal codes so they are specific for your business. For this exercise we are going to select 'Limited Company'.

KAPLAN PUBLISHING

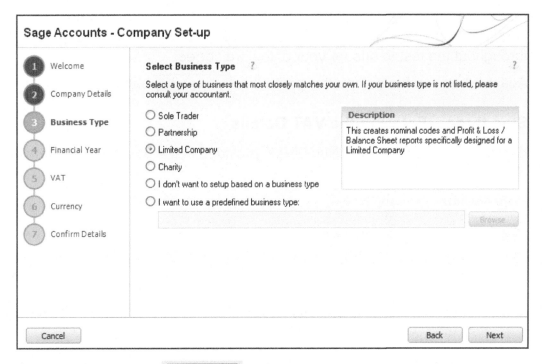

Click the next button [Next]

Step two – Entering the details of the Financial Year

This is a really important stage. You need to enter the dates of your company's Financial Year. Remember, for TotalPhoto Ltd the company's Financial Year is 1st October 2015 to 30th September 2016.

The data in this Study Text all refers to the year 2015-16, and so our Financial Year will start in **October 2015**. Enter this, using the drop down boxes.

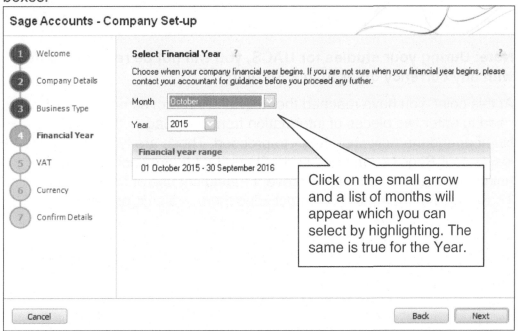

In the real computer based test you will be asked to decide on a suitable year to use based on the dates given. You will need to be consistent throughout the test to ensure your dates are correct.

Again, when you have done this press the [Next] button.

Step three – Entering the VAT Details

Enter the VAT Registration Number as provided in the data (the number is *376096823*).

Step four – Entering the currency details

At this stage you can enter the currency details. All of TotalPhoto Ltd's transactions take place in the UK, so their base currency is "Pound Sterling".

You should check that this option is correctly checked.

Again, click the [Next] button to proceed.

Note: During your studies for UACS, you will not be required to deal with any currency other than £ Sterling.

At this point, you have reached the Activate Program screen. You will now need to enter two pieces of information from your Sage - the Serial Number and the Activation Key - to proceed. These are typically found inside your Sage box marked under "Important Information. These are unique numbers which help to prevent fraudulent use of the software. These are important, and you must keep them in a safe place!

Step five – Confirming the information

At this stage is very important that you check the details you have entered so far. If you are happy with the details on this screen, click

Next to confirm the information.

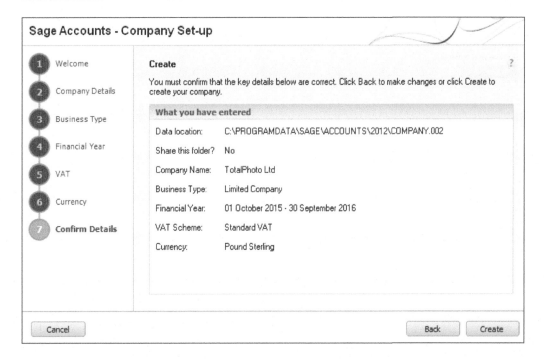

Step six – Active Setup

Well done – you have now set up Sage with the basic information needed for the company TotalPhoto Ltd.

At this stage you can simply press the Create button to move to the next stage.

The name of the company should appear at the top of the screen, with the dates at the bottom, as shown below:

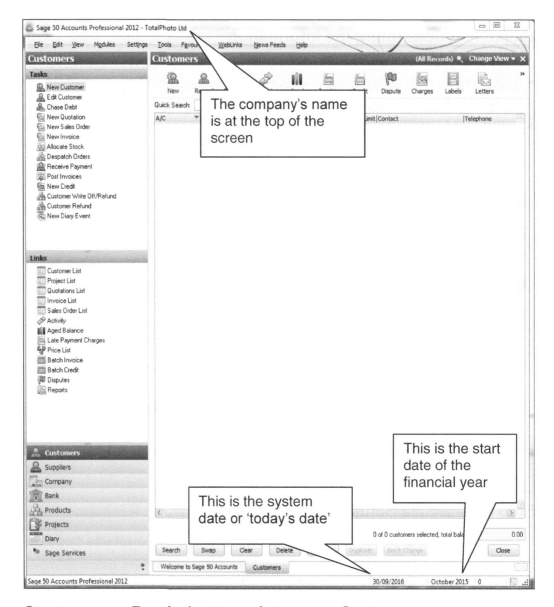

Step seven – Reminder to register your Sage program

In some versions, at this point you may see a notice on screen to remind you to register your copy of Sage. You must do this within **sixty days** of first using the programme. Failure to do this will mean that you are unable to continue using your SAGE software. You can register your product online at www.sage.co.uk or call Sage Customer Services if you require any further assistance with this.

Click [OK   ] to continue.

Navigating Sage

Introduction

You have by now opened your Sage 50 Accounts software and set up the basic details of the company. The next stage is to check your company data and then to practise navigating your way around the different sections of Sage. Don't worry if you have never used a package like Sage before, it is very user-friendly and with lots of practise you will become comfortable with the different functions and areas covered.

ASSESSMENT CRITERIA
Navigating Sage
Produce routine reports from the general ledger (5.2)

CONTENTS	
1	Navigating Sage
2	The customer process screen
3	The supplier process screen
3	Dates
4	Checking your data
5	Making corrections
6	Backing up your work

1 Navigating Sage

This 'window' (or screen) is the one that will now appear every time you open Sage 50 Accounts. You will explore it in more detail as you progress through this Study Text. For now, just take the time to familiarise yourself with this screen.

You can also change the view of the screen to different options by clicking on 'change view' which will be at the top right hand side of your screen.

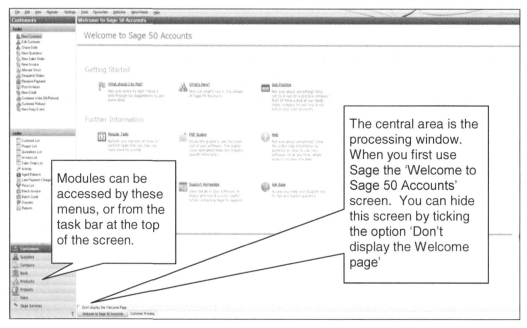

Modules can be accessed by these menus, or from the task bar at the top of the screen.

The central area is the processing window. When you first use Sage the 'Welcome to Sage 50 Accounts' screen. You can hide this screen by ticking the option 'Don't display the Welcome page'

Modules

Sage uses modules to differentiate different transactions. As you move through the different modules, the processing area, tasks, and links will change depending on which module you are working on.

The modules that you will be using for the assessment are: Customers, Suppliers, Company and Bank. The table below identifies the modules you will be using, the accounting term typically used for the module, and the main tasks which are carried out in each module.

Module	Ledger term	Main tasks
Customers	Sales Ledger	• Enter and amend customer details • Enter sales invoices • Enter sales credit notes • Produce invoices and statements • Produce customer reports

Suppliers	Purchase Ledger	• Enter and amend supplier details • Enter purchase invoices • Enter purchase credit notes • Produce supplier reports
Company	Nominal or General ledger	• Enter and amend nominal account records • Produce nominal ledger account reports
Bank	Cash book	• Enter receipts from cash and credit customers • Enter payments to cash and credit suppliers. • Produce reports

You will be exploring these modules in more detail as you work through the case study.

We will now focus on the main screens you will visit throughout your studies and professional use of Sage.

2   The customer process screen

The Customer process screen enables you to access a range of accounting activities connected with your customers.

You can:

• **Post (enter) the details of the invoice onto Sage**

• **Produce a statement showing how much a customer owes you**

• **Receive and account for a payment made by a customer**

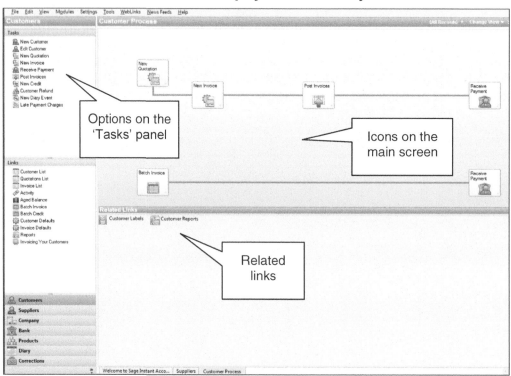

Note that you can access each of these activities in a number of ways.

• The related links tabs at the bottom of the screen

• The options on the 'Tasks' panel

• The icons on the main Customer Process screen

Of course, every business needs customers, but they are not the only aspect of a business. Any business will also need suppliers (of goods, raw materials and services). It will also need a bank account (or maybe more than one!) in which to place its receipts and from which to make payments. Sage allows you to process the transactions relating to these types of activities.

3 The supplier process screen

As with the customer process screen, the supplier process screen enables you to access a range of accounting activities connected with your suppliers.

You can:

- **Post (enter) the details of purchase invoices onto Sage**

- **Post (enter) the details of purchase credit notes onto Sage**

- **Account for payments made to suppliers**

- **Produce supplier reports**

To begin with, click on **Suppliers**

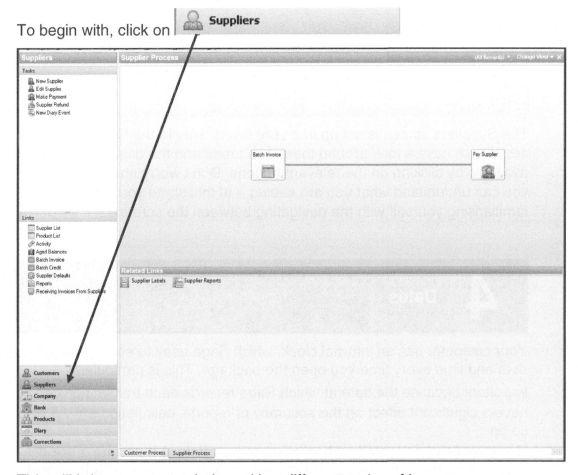

This will bring up a new window with a different series of icons.

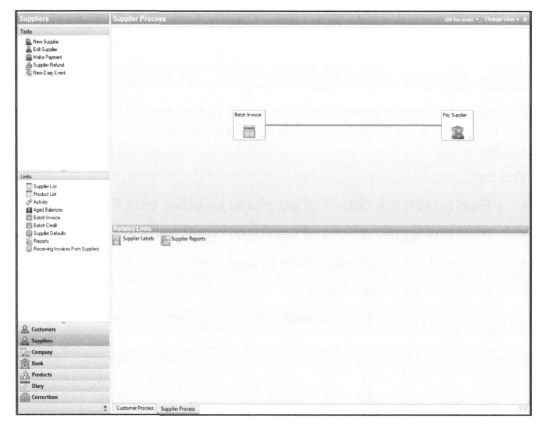

The Suppliers screen is set up in a very similar way to the Customers section, so have a look around these two areas and the different options available by clicking on the relevant buttons. Don't worry about whether you can understand what you are seeing – at this stage you are just familiarising yourself with the navigating between the screens.

4 Dates

Your computer has an internal clock, which Sage uses to set the default date and time every time you open the package. This is particularly important because the date at which Sage records each transaction can have a significant effect on the accuracy of reports, calculation of VAT and so on.

However (and especially when you are practising) it can be a good idea to override this and to enter your own date in line with the case study materials for TotalPhoto Ltd you are about to start working on. If you do this at the start, you will not need to keep re-entering the date when you are entering transactions.

To change the default date

Imagine that you are working on a practise exercise, and you are told that today's date is 30th April 2016. However, the *real date* is 4th December 2016.

The default date in Sage for entering transactions will show as 4th December – and you would have to override this each and every time you made an entry. This is repetitive and increases the likelihood of making a mistake – entering "05" instead of "04", for example.

Fortunately Sage allows you to change the default date. Simply select the 'SETTINGS' menu, and then '**CHANGE PROGRAM DATE**' as shown below:

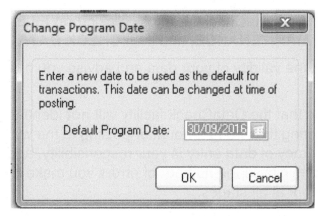

Now you can easily change the date to the date required by the assessment material – in this case 30th September 2016. Now, every time you enter a transaction in SAGE the date will default to 30th September. This will have no effect on your computer's internal clock, and the next time you use the program the default date will revert to the real date once more until you change it.

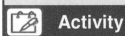 **Activity**

In the TotalPhoto Ltd Case Study, you are told that today's date is 30th September 2016. **You should now change the default date on your computer to 30th September 2016 as detailed above.** Remember that if you subsequently shut Sage down, when you return to it, you will need to change the default date again.

5 Checking your data

If you work steadily and carefully, you should not encounter many problems with your data entry. However, no matter how carefully you work, you will undoubtedly have to make corrections at some time – either because of human error in inputting data, or simply because new information comes to light.

One important feature of Sage is the ability to check your data. This will help to identify any issues with data corruption (which can occur after a power cut, for example), missing data and date errors.

You can access the DataCheck facility by clicking **on FILE** in the main menu bar, then **MAINTENANCE**, and then **CHECK DATA.**

Sage will check the validity of your data and advise you of any possible discrepancies.

You should note that the DataCheck facility will **not** identify data entry errors (e.g. entering the wrong amount or posting to the wrong nominal code). The accuracy of data entry is your responsibility, and you should therefore aim to minimise the number of errors you make by being careful to check your work at all stages.

6 Making corrections

Many people are understandably a little nervous when using a computer system for the first time. They worry that they may break the system, or make mistakes that cannot be corrected.

Don't worry: Sage offers a number of easy ways to amend or delete errors. However, a full record of all amended or deleted transactions are maintained for audit trail purposes.

These are covered in a later chapter so don't panic if you do something wrong. You are only practising at this stage, and it is good to make mistakes initially as you will learn how to correct them! You are allowed to amend errors in the UACS computer based test and will not be penalised for doing so. We all know that mistakes happen in the workplace and errors are often rectified.

 KAPLAN PUBLISHING

7 Backing up your work

It is important that you save your data regularly, to safeguard against accidental losses which can prove very costly and time-consuming to recover or re-input. Backing up your data should become part of your daily routine.

To back up data:

From the File menu at the top of the screen select 'Backup':

Sage now asks if you would like to check your data before you run the backup – you should select [Yes]

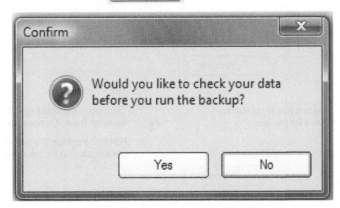

Hopefully there are no problems with your data files and so you will now be able to backup your data.

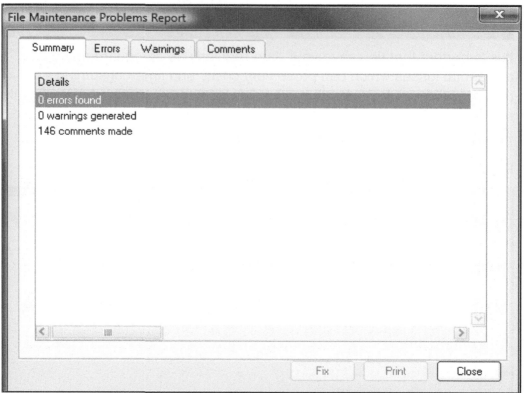

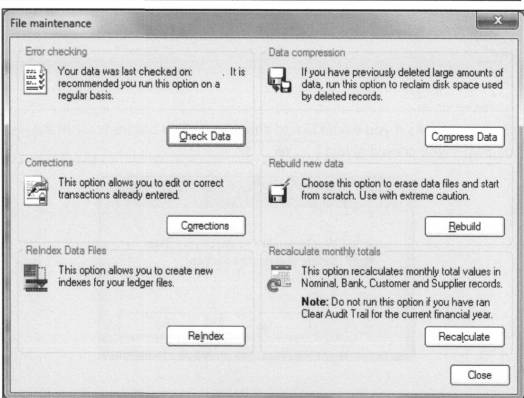

From this screen press the [Close] button to begin backup.

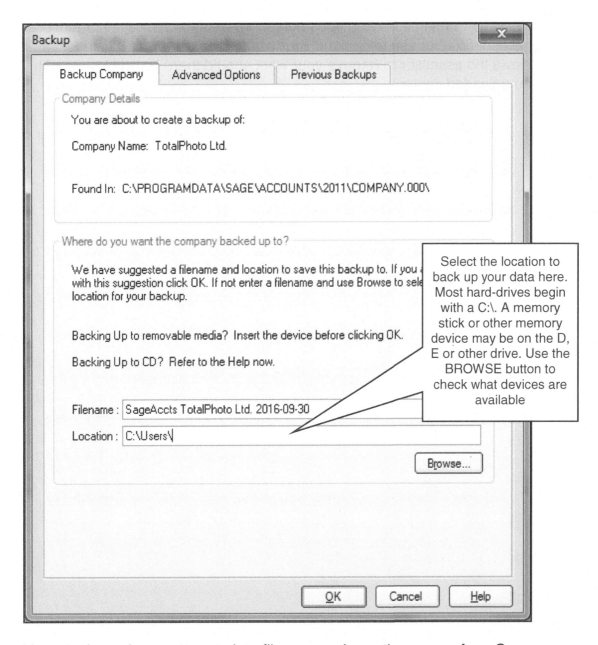

You need to select an appropriate file name – here, the name of our Case Study firm TotalPhoto Ltd has been used. Select **OK** to back up. The screen will now show a "Backup" box which indicates the progress of the backup. Another suggestion for a file name would be to include your name and the date.

When this process has finished Sage will tell you that the backup has been successfully completed and you can click **OK**.

You should note as well that Sage invites you to back up your data each time you close the program down – the process is identical to that described above.

Whilst performing a backup does not form part of the assessment process, it is beneficial for you to back up your work in the computer based test as it allows the assessor to retrieve your work should there be any issues with the uploaded content.

Setting up your suppliers' details

Introduction

Most business organisations will, over time, deal with a wide range of suppliers. For example, a café may have different suppliers for their meat, cheese, vegetables, wine etc. A hairdresser will buy different products from different suppliers. Sometimes supplies will be obtained from a wholesaler or a cash and carry; other supplies may be sourced directly from the manufacturers.

The organisation will need to keep very accurate and timely records of all transactions with their suppliers. These transactions will typically include:

(1)   Purchases and returns

(2)   Discounts received from the supplier

(3)   Payments made to the supplier by cheque or BACS in settlement of outstanding bills

In addition, it would be very convenient to have all the contact details of every supplier easily to hand.

Fortunately Sage provides a very comprehensive supplier management system which covers all these requirements (and more). You will see how this works shortly, but firstly you will need to enter your suppliers' details.

ASSESSMENT CRITERIA	CONTENTS
Set up supplier accounts (1.3)	1 Supplier data
Produce routine reports for customers and suppliers (5.1)	2 Entering supplier data
	3 Printing supplier data reports

1 Supplier data

We can now start inputting some data on to the computerised system using our case study firm, TotalPhoto Ltd.

 Activity

TotalPhoto Ltd has six suppliers, whose details are given below. Enter these onto the computerised system. Guidance on how to enter these records for suppliers follows.

Supplier details

Mackay Films Ltd	**A/c Ref : MF001**

33 West Parade
Miltonby
Lancashire
LN87 7HD

Tel 01828 827493

Contact: Carl Richardson

Outstanding Balance at 30th September 2015: **£345.36**

Credit Terms: **30 days**	**Credit Limit £2,500**

K2 Films Ltd	**A/c Ref : KF001**

Tokyo House
72-84 Great Milne Street
London
WC4 6DD

Tel 0207 867 6599

Contact: Kim Nakajima

Outstanding Balance at 30th September 2015: **£1,726.55**

Credit Terms: **30 days**	**Credit Limit £5,000**

The Stationery Cupboard   **A/c Ref : SC003**

21 Potter Way
Hull
Humberside
HU87 6YY

Tel 01482 417378

Contact: Alan Pensill

Outstanding Balance at 30th September 2015: **£375.00**

Credit Terms: **14 days**   **Credit Limit £1,000**

Mills Paper Products   **A/c Ref : MP002**

405 Ream Road
Bradford
West Yorkshire
BD5 6QA

Tel 01726 378918

Contact: Mr Shaun Squire

Outstanding Balance at 30th September 2015: **£4,920.30**

Credit Terms: **21 days,**   **Credit Limit £8,000**

Octopus Inks Ltd   **A/c Ref : OI001**

Unit 12
Longley Industrial Park
Gateshead
Tyne and Wear
GH77 5TG

Tel 0191 252 4132

Contact: Sheila Cribbley

Outstanding Balance at 30th September 2015: **£550.20**

Credit Terms: **30 days**   **Credit Limit £2,500**

Arthur's Photographic Equipment Ltd	**A/c Ref : AP004**

77 Overton Lane
Birmingham
BM97 8YK

Tel 0121 299 0192

Contact: Jennie Reeves

Outstanding Balance at 30th September 2015: **£11,275.00**

Credit Terms: **30 days**	**Credit Limit £20,000**

2 Entering supplier data

Now you need to set up your suppliers by entering the details from the activity. All balances will need to be set up using the date of 1st October 2015 as this is the first day of your accounting period.

From the Supplier Process window (below) select the new supplier wizard by clicking on either **New Supplier** in the Tasks list, or on the New Supplier icon.

This will bring up the **Supplier Record Wizard**, which will help you to easily enter your suppliers' details.

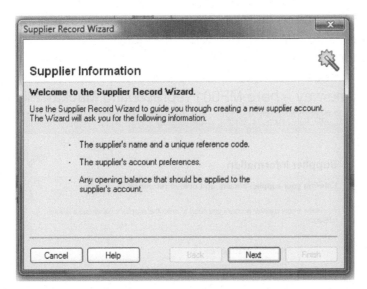

To continue with this you will need to refer to the list of suppliers for TotalPhoto Ltd detailed within the activity on the previous pages.

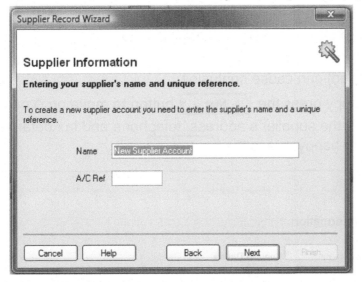

The first supplier to enter is:

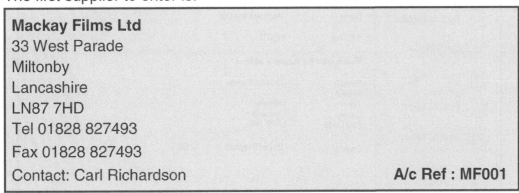

Mackay Films Ltd
33 West Parade
Miltonby
Lancashire
LN87 7HD
Tel 01828 827493
Fax 01828 827493
Contact: Carl Richardson   **A/c Ref : MF001**

To complete the first screen of the **New Supplier Wizard** you will need to enter the supplier's name (Mackay Films Ltd) and their unique Account Reference Number (A/C Ref – MF001).

The Account Reference Number is a shorthand way of identifying each of your suppliers. You can use this code on documentation, and also it will appear on reports that you will print out. It is extremely important that the number you choose is unique and it is useful if it helps to identify the supplier in some way – here MF001 representing **M**ackay **F**ilms.

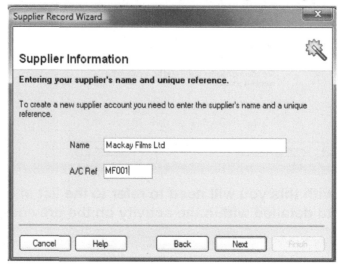

It is important to check your spelling for accuracy as errors (although they can be rectified) can cause confusion.

If you are happy press the [Next] button to move on. You will now need to enter the supplier's address, telephone and fax details. Again, when you are happy, press the [Next]

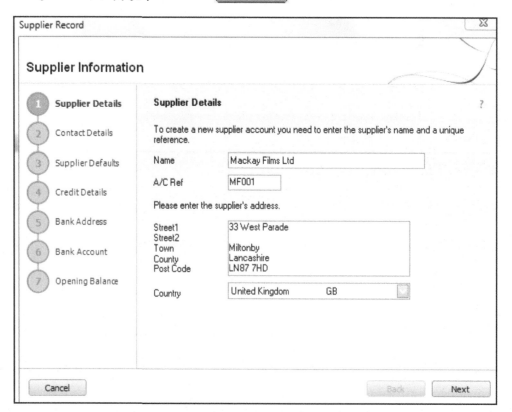

Now you can enter the firm's contact details. In this case we have not got an e-mail or website address, or the VAT number. Don't worry, though, as these can easily be entered at a later date.

You can enter Carl Richardson's name at this point, though, before pressing the [Next] button.

The next screen asks you to enter details of any discount available from this supplier, the nominal code against which purchases from this supplier will be recorded, and also the most common VAT rating for the goods that you buy from them.

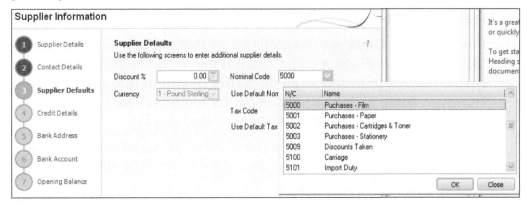

Mackay Films Ltd do not offer any discount, so this can be left at **0.00.**

The firm supplies films to TotalPhoto, so the Nominal Code should be 5000 (you will learn more about nominal codes later). The VAT code is T1, meaning that the majority of purchases from this supplier will have VAT added at 20%.

If you are happy with this press the [Next] button.

The next screen allows you to enter details of any credit terms that the supplier offers. Most suppliers will insist on payment within a certain period of time – typically seven to thirty days **(the payment due days)**. However, some suppliers may also offer a discount for payment within an earlier period **(the settlement due days).**

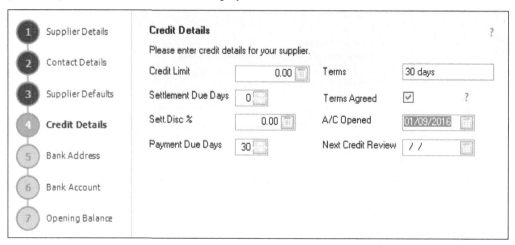

- **Credit limit** is the amount of credit allowed by this supplier. Here we can enter the credit limit agreed with the supplier, in this case £2500.

- **Settlement Due Days and Sett. Disc**% relate to any extra discount allowed by the supplier if the invoice is paid within a certain time. In this instance, no settlement (or cash) discount has been given, so **leave both these boxes as zero**

- **Payment Due Days** are the credit terms that the supplier offers. Most suppliers will insist on payment within a certain period of time – typically seven to twenty eight days **(the payment due days).** However, some suppliers may also offer a discount for payment within an earlier period **(the settlement due days)**.

  Mackay Films Ltd offer credit terms of **30 days** meaning TotalPhoto Ltd must pay invoices within 30 days after the invoice date.

- **Terms** Enter the terms agreed as text: 30 days

- **Terms agreed** You will also want to tick this box, as this tells Sage that the details have been confirmed. If you forget to do this at this particular stage, don't worry as you can choose to tick terms agreed by double clicking on the particular supplier in the **SUPPLIERS** module, and then clicking on the 'credit control' tab.

- **A/C Opened** For this Case Study we are working in the month of September, 2016. Any new accounts opened this month will be dated the 1st September, 2016.

If you are happy with this press the [Next] button.

The next screens ask you to enter the details of your supplier's bank. This is essential if the business is paying their suppliers using methods such as BACS. It is not necessary for you to do this in this example and you will not be required to enter information of this nature in your AAT computer based test.

An example of information that could be entered at this stage is given below:

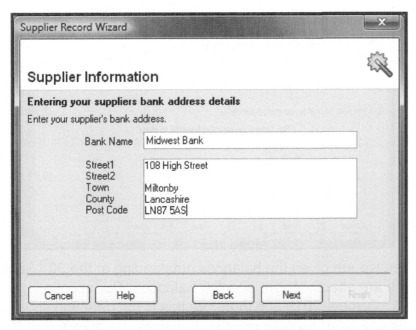

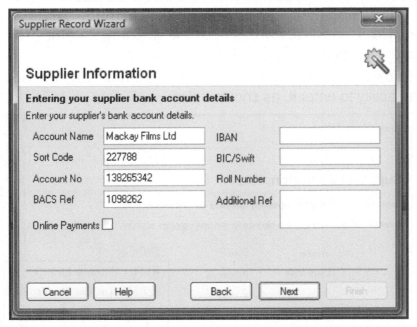

Sage now asks if this supplier has an outstanding balance – in other words, if at the time of entering their details you already owe them money. In this example, TotalPhoto Ltd currently owes Mackay Films Ltd £345.36. This figure can be entered either as one figure by selecting 'Yes, as one value'.

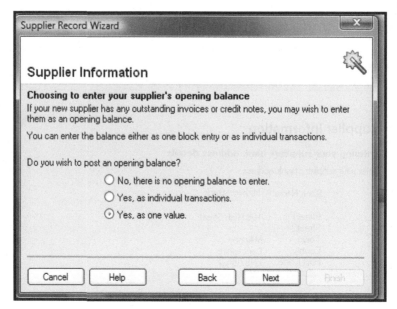

Remember, we are given the balances outstanding at the 30th September 2015 which are effectively our opening balances. Our accounting year starts on 1st October 2015 and therefore this is the date you should enter when setting up your supplier opening balances. **Be aware that the date to use for opening balances usually differs to 'today's date' given in the scenario. Therefore, always read the wording carefully to ensure you use the correct date.**

On the following screen either type the date (01/10/2015) or use Sage's calendar facility to enter it, as shown below.

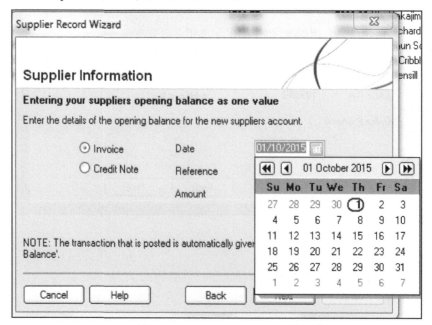

You can now also enter the opening balance for Mackay Films Ltd. Check your entries then press the [Next] button.

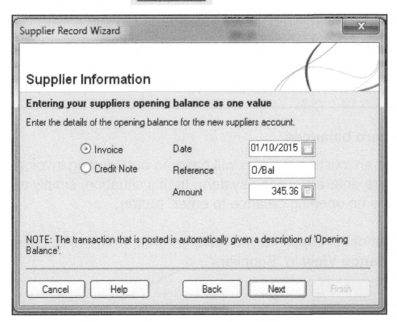

Well done! You have now entered your first supplier details. To recap, you began by entering their company details, such as their address, phone and fax numbers and contact details. Then you entered the credit terms that this supplier makes available, including normal payment terms and any discounts that are available for early settlement. After that, you entered your supplier's bank details and finally the opening balance of debt to that supplier.

Sage now confirms that you have successfully entered the supplier's details. The next stage is important – you **must** press the [Finish] button to save the details and to post the opening balance.

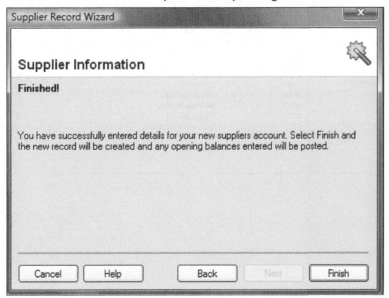

Activity

You have already entered one of TotalPhoto Ltd's suppliers (Mackay Films Ltd).

You should now enter the full details for each of the remaining five suppliers, and then save them to SAGE.

Entering zero balances

Sometimes an existing supplier will have no outstanding invoices at the date they are entered into the system. In this situation, simply click on the "No, there is no opening balance to enter" button.

To see a list of the suppliers you have entered, from the Supplier Process window **Change View** to 'Suppliers'.

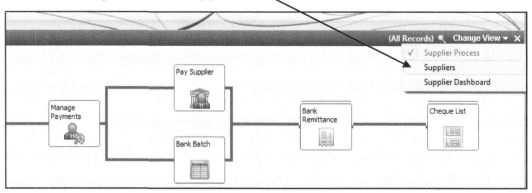

Your list of suppliers should look like this:

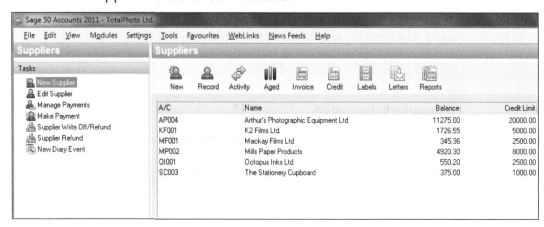

Contact information should have also been completed:

Contact	Telephone
Jennie Reeves	0121 299 0192
Kim Nakajima	0207 8676599
Carl Richardson	01828 827493
Mr Shaun Squire	01726 378918
Sheila Cribbley	0191 252 4132
Alan Pensill	01482 417378

If you spot a mistake, you can go into the Supplier Record by clicking on the Record icon and making the necessary corrections.

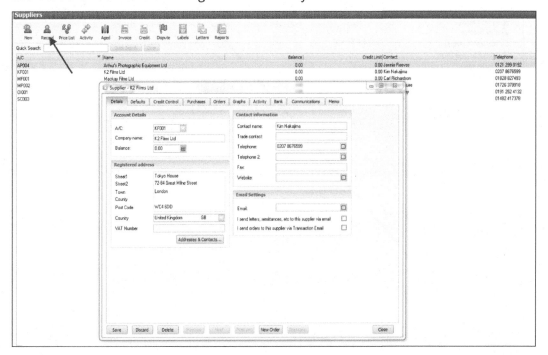

3 Printing supplier data reports

You have entered the details of the six suppliers, so let's now check that they are correct by running off a report from Sage.

The first report to print is the Supplier List.

From the **Suppliers** window (shown below), click on **Reports** in the **Links** area or the **Reports** icon.

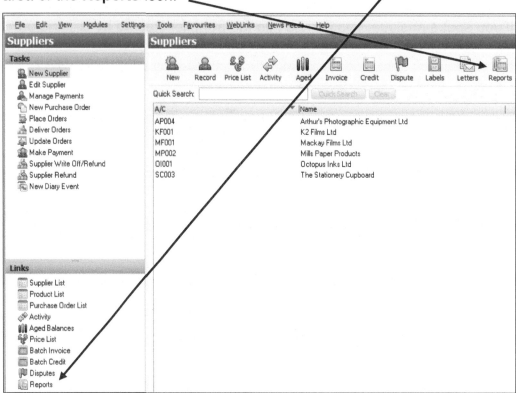

This will produce a new window with a list of supplier-related reports that you could want to print and use. You will practise accessing some more of these later on, but for now the one that you want is the report entitled **Supplier Address List**. This is contained within the folder called *Supplier Details Reports* – to access the contents of this (or any) folder simply click on the + sign to the side of the folder name to expand it to show its contents.

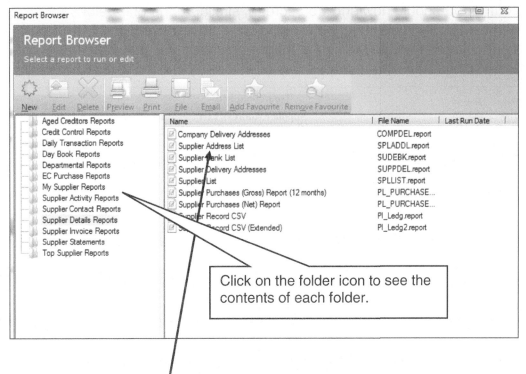

Double click on **Supplier Address List** to produce the report.

On the next screen you can identify the criteria by which you wish to select the contents of your report. As you wish to see a list of all the suppliers that you have entered keep the boxes as shown below, then press OK.

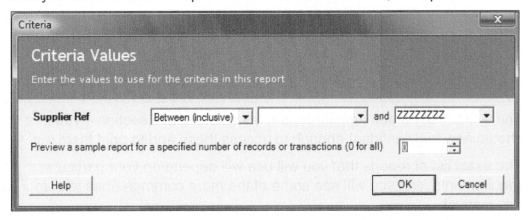

Your report should now show on screen, similar to the one below. Remember, that you might be working on a different version of Sage but the main areas will be the same but possibly with a slightly different presentation.

| Date: | 24/08/2016 | **TotalPhoto Ltd.** | | Page: | 1 |
| Time: | 23:35:25 | **Supplier Address List** | | | |

Supplier From:
Supplier To: ZZZZZZZZ

A/C	Name	Contact	Telephone	Fax
AP004	Arthur's Photographic Equipment Ltd. 77 Overton Lane Birmingham BM97 8YK	Jennie Reeves	0121 299 0192	
KF001	K2 Films Ltd. Tokyo House 72 - 84 Great Milne Street Lodon WC4 6DD	Kim Nakajima	0207 867 6599	
MF001	Mackay Films Ltd 33 West Parade Miltonby Lancashire LN87 7HD	Carl Richardson	01828 827 493	
MP002	Mills Paper Products 405 Ream Road Bradford West Yorkshire BD5 6QA	Mr Shaun Squire	01726 378 918	
OI001	Octopus Inks Ltd Unit 12 Longley Industrial Park Gateshead Tynne and Wear GH77 5TG	Sheila Cribbley	0191 252 4132	
SC003	The Stationery Cupboard 21 Potter Way Hull Humberside HU87 6YY	Alan Pensill	01482 417378	

There are many other supplier reports available in this section – you should now feel confident enough to access these and to print them out.

The exact list of reports that you will use will depend on your particular requirements, and you will see some of the more common ones later in this manual.

You will feel much more comfortable in generating reports once you have practised, so have a go!

Setting up your customers' details

Introduction

Now that you have successfully entered your suppliers' details you can now move on to enter relevant information about your customers as well.

The process of entering your customers' details is very similar to that of entering supplier information, so you should feel confident doing this now.

It is of course vitally important that you keep accurate records for each of your customers. This information is likely to include:

(1) Sales made on credit to customers, and sales returns

(2) Credit terms for your customers, including any discount they may receive

(3) Contact details for easy invoicing

(4) Payments received from customers

Consistent, accurate recording of information is a vital aspect of any credit management system, ensuring that your organisation gets paid as quickly as possible for its sales. This can be the difference between failure and survival for most businesses.

ASSESSMENT CRITERIA	CONTENTS
Set up customer accounts, entering opening balances where appropriate (1.2)	1 Customer data
	2 Entering customer data
Produce routine reports for customers and suppliers (5.1)	3 Printing customer data reports

1 Customer data

The process of entering your customers' details is very similar to that of entering supplier information, so you should feel confident doing this now.

Consistent, accurate recording of information is a vital aspect of any credit management system, ensuring that your organisation gets paid as quickly as possible for its sales. This can be the difference between failure and survival for most businesses.

We can now start to look at the 'Customers' process and begin with entering the initial information regarding our case study firm, TotalPhoto Ltd. Again, you will find detailed step by step instructions directly after this activity.

 Activity

TotalPhoto Ltd has six customers with outstanding balances as at 30th September 2015. Their details and guidance on how to enter the customer details follow.

Mr W Haslam
22 Brown Street
Miltonby
Lancashire LN87 6FD
A/c Ref : HAS004

Amount outstanding at 30th September 2015: £309.85

Credit terms: Payment in 14 days   Credit limit: £500

Mrs H Poppy
120 Forrest Way
Miltonby
Lancashire LN87 9YR
A/c Ref : POP002

Amount outstanding at 30th September 2015: £220.00

Credit terms: Payment in 14 days   Credit limit: £500

Mrs T Pashby
30A Andrews Street
Killington
Lancashire LN85 6TT
A/c Ref: PAS002

Amount outstanding at 30th September 2015:   £89.50

Credit terms: Payment in 14 days   Credit limit: £500

Campbell & Dunn Ltd
12 The Beeches
Miltonby
Lancashire LN87 9PP
A/c Ref: CAM004

Amount outstanding at 30th September 2015:   £2056.85

Credit terms: Payment in 14 days   Credit limit: £2500

Lullabies Nursery
104 Victoria Road
Miltonby
Lancashire LN87 5PS
A/c Ref: LUL002

Amount outstanding at 30th September 2015:   £726.90

Credit terms: Payment in 14 days   Credit limit: £1500

Miss S Pargenter
11 Alexandra Park
Miltonby
Lancashire LN87 2WD
A/c Ref: PAR006

Amount outstanding at 30th September 2015:   £650.00

Credit terms: Payment in 14 days   Credit limit: £1000

You will now enter these six customer details into Sage.

2 Entering customer data

Now you need to set up your customers by entering the customer details from the activity. All balances will need to be set up using the date of 1st October 2015 as this is the first day of your accounting period.

Go to the Customer Process screen, as below.

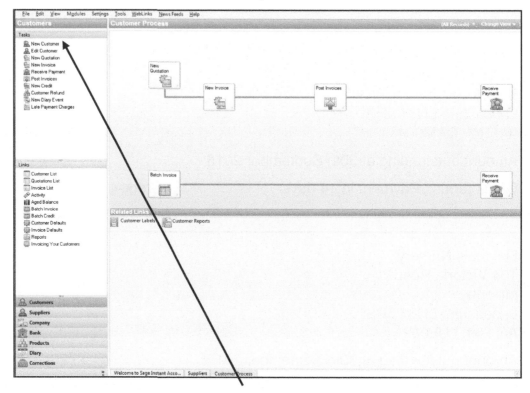

From the Task Bar, click on **New Customer**. At the next screen click NEXT, and you should now be able to enter your first customer's details, as below.

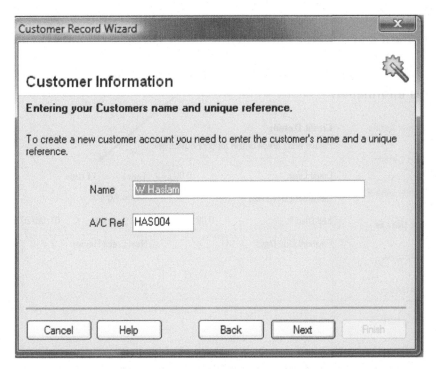

When you have done this click the **NEXT** button again, and enter the address details, as below.

As with the supplier entry process, the next screen will ask you for further contact details, such as email and website addresses. You do not need to enter any information here at this point, so press the **NEXT** button.

Now you can enter the credit terms for this customer.

For Mr Haslam we will require payment within fourteen days, and there is no settlement discount for early payment. Mr Haslam opened his account on 01/09/2016.

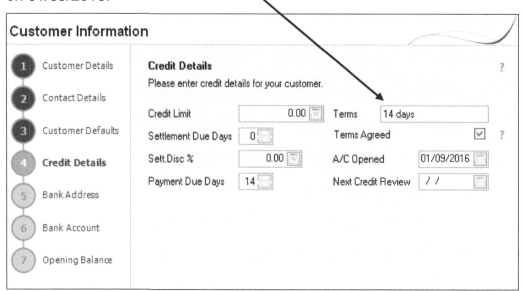

The credit limit represents the maximum value of goods or services we are prepared to sell to them on credit. Here, for Mr Haslam, it is £500.

As with the supplier process, you will also need to tick the 'Terms Agreed' box, as this tells Sage that the details have been confirmed. If you forget to do this at this particular stage, don't worry as you can choose to tick terms agreed by double clicking on the particular customer in the CUSTOMERS module, and then clicking on the 'credit control' tab.

Be careful to enter all information accurately and correctly at every stage of this process – check that the details you have entered match the source data.

Sage will now ask if there are any opening balances, and as with the supplier entry screen you should choose to enter them as a single value.

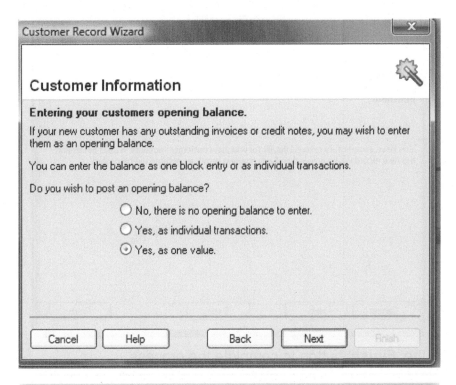

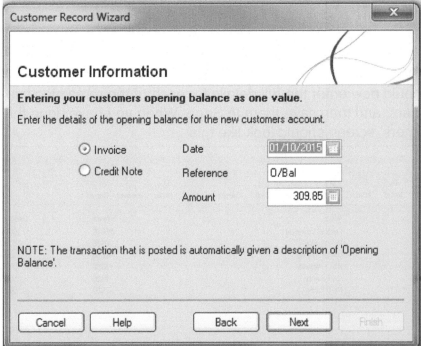

Enter the opening balance for Mr Haslam (£309.85) as above.

Sage now asks you to confirm the details you have entered and to save them. Again, this is an important stage of the process.

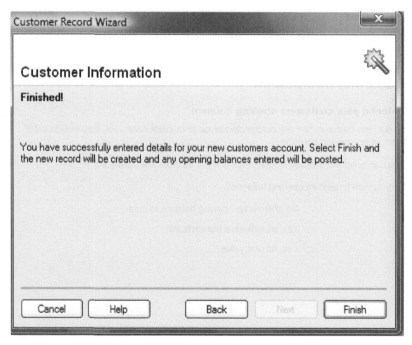

Click on the '**Finish**' button to complete the process.

Activity

You have already entered one of TotalPhoto Ltd's customers (Mr W Haslam).

You should now enter the full details for each of the remaining five customers, and then save them to Sage. When you have done this, your 'Customers' screen should look like this:

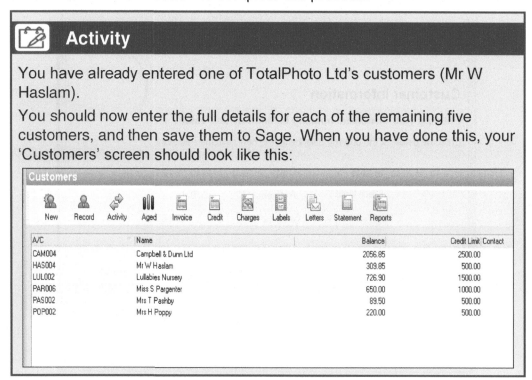

3 Printing customer data reports

You have entered the details of the six customers, so let's now check that they are correct by running off a report from Sage.

The first report to print is the Customer List.

From the **Customers** window (shown below), click on **Reports** in the **Links** area.

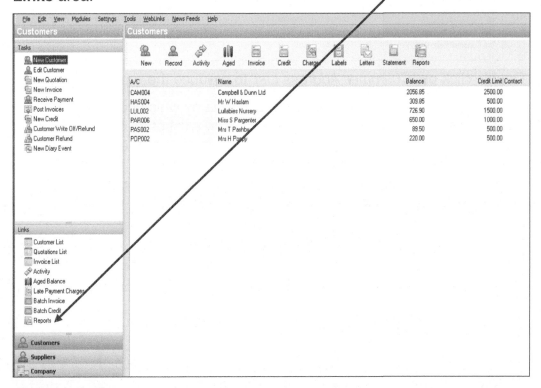

This will produce a new window with a list of customer-related reports that you may want to print and use. You will practice accessing some more of these later on, but for now the one that you want is the report entitled *Customer Address List*.

This is contained within the folder called *Customer Details Reports* – to access the contents of this (or any) folder simply click on the folder icon.

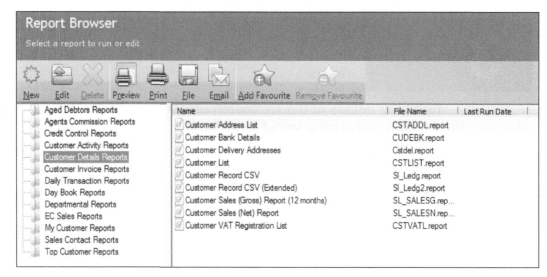

Double click on '*Customer Address List*' to produce the report.

On the next screen you can identify the criteria by which you wish to select the contents of your report. As you wish to see a list of all of the customers that you have entered keep the boxes as shown below, then press OK.

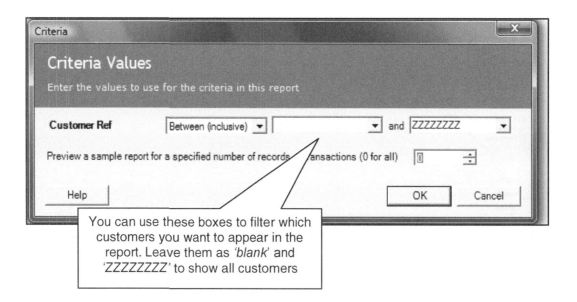

Your report should now show on screen, similar to the one below.

Date: 28/08/2016	**TotalPhoto Ltd.**		**Page:** 1
Time: 11:16:50	**Customer Address List**		

Customer From:
Customer To: *ZZZZZZZZ*

A/C	Name & Address	Contact Name	Telephone	Fax
CAM004	Campbell & Dunn 12 The Beaches Miltonby Lancashire LN87 9PP			
HAS004	Mr W Haslam 22 Brown Street Miltonby Lancashire LN87 6FD			
LUL002	Lullabies Nursery 104 Victoria Road Miltonby Lancashire LN87 5PS			
PAR006	Miss S Pargenter 11 Alexandra Park Miltonby Lancashire LN87 2WD			
PAS002	Mrs T Pashby 30A Andrews Street Killington Lancashire LN85 6TT			
POP002	Mrs H Poppy 120 Forrest Way Miltonby Lancashire LN87 9YR			

There are many other customer reports available in this section – you should now feel confident enough to access these and to print them out. The exact list of reports that you will use will depend on your particular requirements, and you will see some of the more common ones later in this manual.

The nominal ledger

7

ASSESSMENT CRITERIA

Enter information relating to the organisation at the beginning of an accounting period (1.1)

Produce routine reports from the general ledger (5.2)

CONTENTS

1 Introduction
2 Set up and amend general ledger accounts
3 Enter the relevant opening balance information
4 Printing a trial balance

1 Introduction

The nominal ledger is probably the most important element of the SAGE (or indeed any) accounting system. The key aspect to this is the list of nominal codes. This is simply a series of different accounts which are used each time a transaction is recorded.

Each of these accounts is given a unique four digit code number. To view the list of Nominal Codes go to the **COMPANY** screen, and then **NOMINAL LEDGER.**

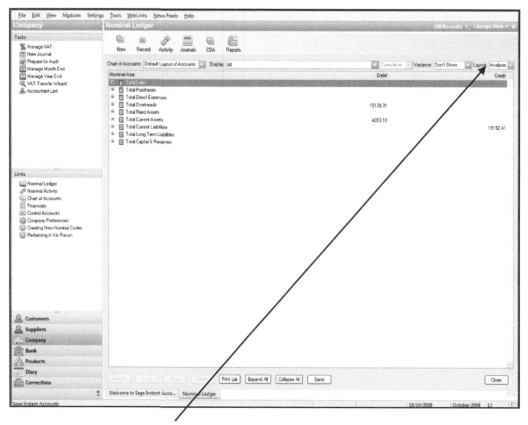

Select 'List' from the layout menu.

This now shows you a list of all of the nominal codes (N/Cs) for the business (ignore any figures shown above as they are for demonstration purposes only).

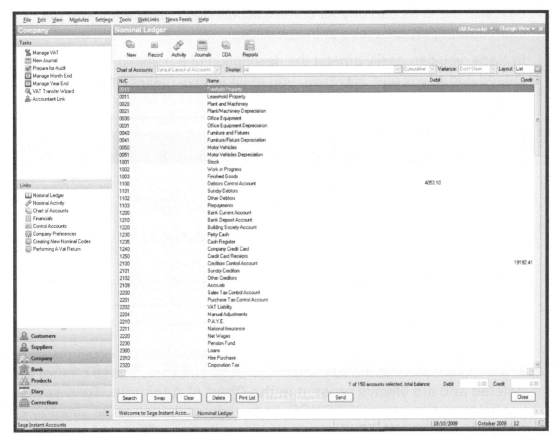

The four-digit code is important, as the list is actually broken down into groups:

0000-0999	Fixed Assets and Depreciation (e.g. Buildings, Equipment)
1000-1999	Current Assets (e.g. Stock, Debtors, Bank)
2000-2999	Liabilities (e.g. Loans, Creditors)
3000-3999	Capital and Reserves
4000-4999	Sales
5000-5999	Purchases
6000-6999	Direct Expenses (e.g. Direct Labour)
7000-7999	Miscellaneous Overheads (e.g. Phone, Rent, Postage)
8000-8999	Bad debts and Depreciation
9000-9999	Suspense and Mispostings

Sage uses these 'groupings' of codes to ensure that items appear in the correct part of the Income Statement or Statement of Financial Position. You may have heard of these financial statements referred to as a 'Profit and Loss Account' or 'Balance Sheet'. Don't worry you will not have to deal with these as part of your current accounting qualification and will learn how to prepare these at the next level.

In Sage, you can easily amend the description of a nominal code, or indeed add a new one. However, you must always make sure that you keep the code in the correct 'grouping' for the type of account that it is.

 Activity

You should now print out the list of nominal codes. Do this by simply pressing the [Print List] button located towards the bottom of the screen. The full list of default Nominal Codes should now print.

You should now keep this list safe, as you will need to use it when entering transactions in the future.

Control accounts

There are some very special Nominal Codes called Control Accounts, which are essential to the running of the Sage software. **These cannot be deleted and are always present in the Chart of Accounts.** To view the control accounts, go to **SETTINGS** *(in the tabs at the top of the screen)* – **CONTROL ACCOUNTS**. This will show you the main Control Accounts within Sage, as shown next.

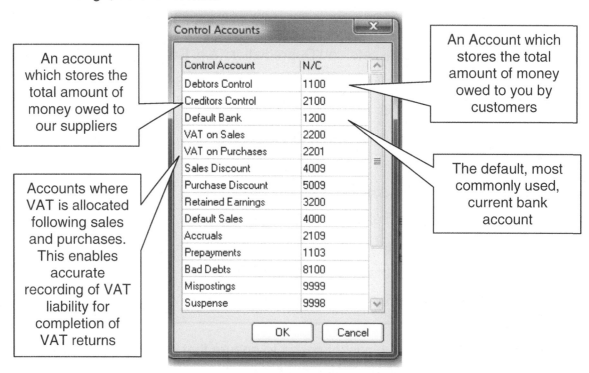

An account which stores the total amount of money owed to our suppliers

An Account which stores the total amount of money owed to you by customers

Accounts where VAT is allocated following sales and purchases. This enables accurate recording of VAT liability for completion of VAT returns

The default, most commonly used, current bank account

Control Account	N/C
Debtors Control	1100
Creditors Control	2100
Default Bank	1200
VAT on Sales	2200
VAT on Purchases	2201
Sales Discount	4009
Purchase Discount	5009
Retained Earnings	3200
Default Sales	4000
Accruals	2109
Prepayments	1103
Bad Debts	8100
Mispostings	9999
Suspense	9998

Most of these accounts are used automatically by Sage. This means that you do not need to specify them individually when entering transaction.

Sage will work out which control account is required and apply it automatically. Other Nominal Codes (from the list you printed out) will need to be entered.

2 Set up and amend general ledger accounts

The default Chart of Accounts contains the most common codes set up for a general business. However, you will almost certainly want to add to, or amend, these Nominal Codes to suit your business in particular.

For example, in your case study TotalPhoto Ltd you will want to be more specific when recording its sales and purchases. Before you do this, have a look at your listing of Nominal Codes. Find the 5000-5999 Range (remember, these are set aside for Purchases).

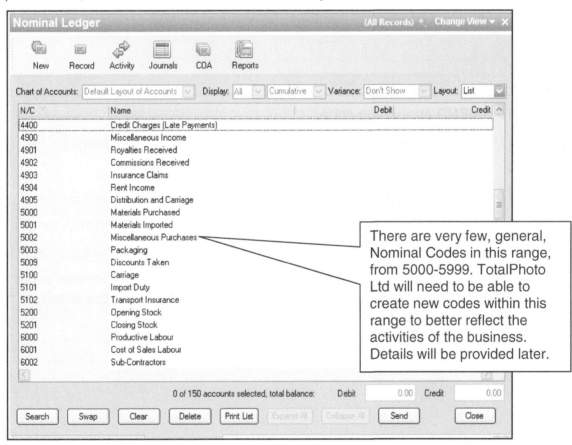

Now, from within the NOMINAL module click on the Record button.

You should now have a blank record screen, as below.

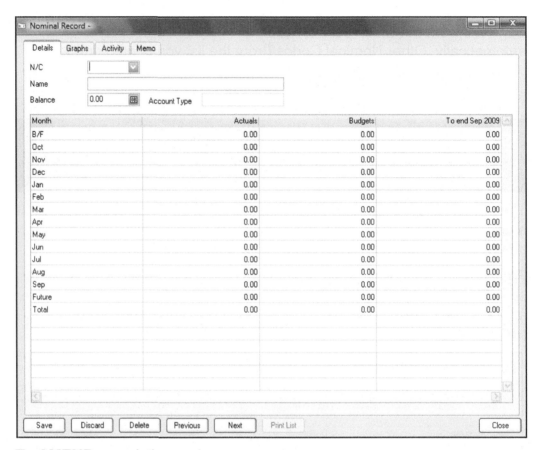

To **AMEND** an existing code:

- Enter the Nominal Code (or select from the pull down menu)

- Type in the new name

To **CREATE** a new code:

- Enter the new Nominal Code (making sure it is in the correct range)

- Type in the new name

There is also the option of using a 'wizard' to set up a new nominal code. It is a very straightforward process and it guides you through the relevant steps. To do this, click on '**Company'** and then '**New**'.

Activity

To practise amending and creating Nominal Codes, enter each of the following N/Cs and names. Do them one by one, and then save each one. These are all relevant to our case study firm – TotalPhoto Ltd.

SALES		PURCHASES	
Nominal Code	*Name*	*Nominal Code*	*Name*
4000	Sales – Individuals & Family	5000	Purchases – Film
4001	Sales – Weddings	5001	Purchases – Paper
4002	Sales – Corporate	5002	Purchases – Cartridges & Toner
4003	Sales – Nurseries & Schools	5003	Purchases – Stationery
4004	Other sales	5004	Purchases – Other Consumables

Once you have created and amended the nominal codes from the previous activity, close down the window and generate the Nominal List report for the range 4000-5999.

This should now look like this:

Date: 02/07/2013   **TotalPhoto Ltd**   Page: 1
Time: 12:33:56   **Nominal List**

N/C From: 4000
N/C To: 5999

N/C	Name
4000	Sales - Individuals & Family
4001	Sales - Weddings
4002	Sales - Corporate
4003	Sales - Nurseries & Schools
4004	Other Sales
4009	Discounts Allowed
4099	Flat Rate - Benefit/Cost
4100	Sales Type D
4101	Sales Type E
4200	Sales of Assets
4400	Credit Charges (Late Payments)
4900	Miscellaneous Income
4901	Royalties Received
4902	Commissions Received
4903	Insurance Claims
4904	Rent Income
4905	Distribution and Carriage
5000	Purchases - Film
5001	Purchases - Paper
5002	Purchases - Cartridges & Toner
5003	Purchases - Stationery
5004	Purchases - Other Consumables
5009	Discounts Taken
5100	Carriage
5101	Import Duty
5102	Transport Insurance
5200	Opening Stock
5201	Closing Stock

Note the new sales categories here

Note the new purchases categories here

Well done! Now you can amend or create new nominal codes. The next step is to post opening balances to each relevant nominal code within Sage for your business.

Activity

You now need to enter the opening balances for each of the accounts relating to TotalPhoto Ltd. You need to enter the financial balance on each account for TotalPhoto Ltd. This needs to be the first date you begin using the Sage system to record financial transactions for the company. Just as with the customers and suppliers, you are to enter all opening balances as at 1st October 2015. The list of opening balances is shown below and **detailed guidance on how to enter these balances follow this activity:**

Important

1   You will need to create new Nominal Codes for two items: Photographic Equipment and Photographic Equipment Depreciation (use Plant & Machinery as the category when setting up the new codes). You may also choose to re-name the nominal account called Ordinary Shares (no 3000) to Capital – Ordinary Shares although this is optional. These need entering/updating **before** going to the opening balances screen.

2   You do not need to enter opening balances for two items, the Debtors Control Account and the Creditors Control Account. This is because these represent the total amount owed to us (debtors/receivables) and the total amount we owe (creditors/payables), made up of all of the individual balances you entered earlier. These control account balances are therefore calculated automatically by SAGE and **you do not enter them.**

3   Be very careful to enter each balance correctly as either a **debit** or a **credit** balance. Take your time to complete this activity as it will prevent errors at this stage.

4   Remember you can edit any of the account names and create any relevant nominal codes. It is recommended that you run through the nominal codes and names before you enter the opening balances to ensure that the details are as you want them to be.

TotalPhoto Ltd

Opening Balances

	Nominal code	Debit	Credit
Motor vehicles (at cost)	0050	21800.00	
Motor Vehicles Depreciation	0051		5450.00
Office Equipment	0030	4849.00	
Office Equipment Depreciation	0031		921.00
Photographic Equipment	0032	22718.00	
Photographic Equip Depreciation	0033		4316.00
Stock (as at 1st October 2015)	1001	7403.00	
Petty Cash	1230	250.00	
Bank	1200	10293.00	
Creditors Control Account	2100		19192.41
Capital – Ordinary Shares	3000		20000.00
Purchases – Film	5000	205.63	
Purchases – Paper	5001	1034.35	
Purchases – Cartridges & Toner	5002	1225.87	
Purchases – Stationery	5003	409.35	
Purchases – Other Consumables	5004	823.52	
Sales – Individuals & Families	4000		5401.21
Sales – Weddings	4001		3984.50
Sales – Corporate	4002		1932.09
Sales – Nurseries & Schools	4003		11304.20
Other Sales	4004		1590.30
Rent	7100	3800.00	
Rates	7103	480.00	
Telephone	7502	603.43	
Motor expenses	7304	1035.64	
Miscellaneous expenses	6900	229.39	
Debtors Control Account	1100	4053.10	
Retained profits	3200		5498.28
VAT	2202		1623.29
		81213.28	**81213.28**

Note: this is the total of the suppliers' balances that you entered earlier. This has already been entered and so will not need to be entered again

Similarly this is the total of the individual customers' accounts that you entered earlier. Again, this will not need to be entered again

3 Enter the relevant opening balance information

Entering a new balance

Entering opening balances in Sage is very straightforward. If you enter an opening balance incorrectly, please refer to a later chapter for detailed guidance on how to correct.

From the main screen click on the '**Company**' button. This will bring up the Nominal Ledger screen, as shown below.

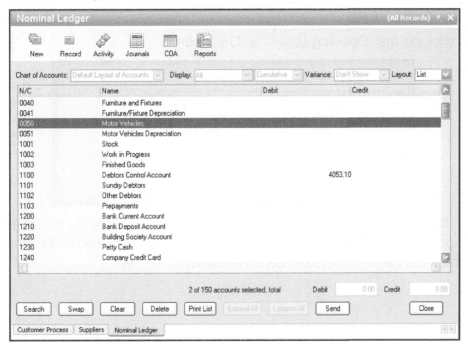

Highlight the Nominal Code for which you want to enter an opening balance.

The first amount we need to enter is for Motor Vehicles – the amount is £21,800 (debit balance). You can see that the Motor Vehicles account has been automatically assigned a Nominal Code of **0050** by Sage.

Double-click your mouse on this code.

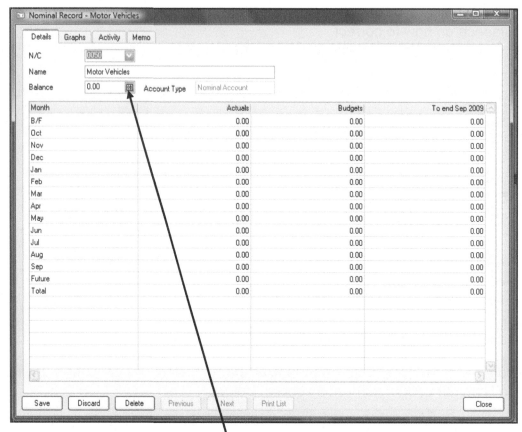

Now click on the 'Opening Balance (**OB**)' icon.

Keep the Ref as "O/Bal". Change the date box to 01/10/2015, and enter the opening balance amount of £21,800.00 in the Debit box. Leave the credit box at zero. Then click the Save button.

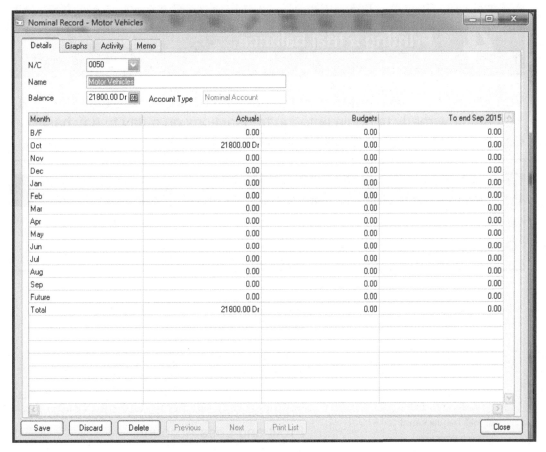

Notice how the detail record for Nominal Code 0050 (Motor Vehicles) has now changed, showing your entry in September. When you return to the Nominal Ledger page you should also see the new balance reflected there.

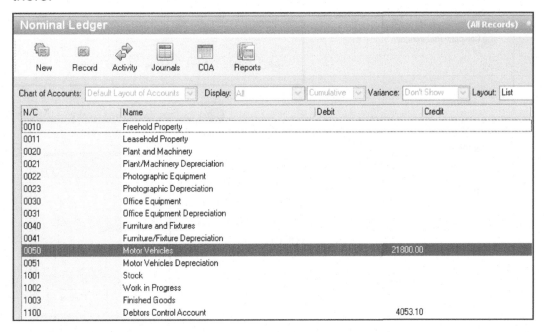

4 Printing a trial balance

You should now have entered all the opening balances for TotalPhoto Ltd. You are now ready to begin entering transactions on a day to day basis. Before you do this, you should print off a Trial Balance.

 Activity

Print off a trial balance for TotalPhoto Ltd as at 1st October 2015. Guidance on how to do this follows.

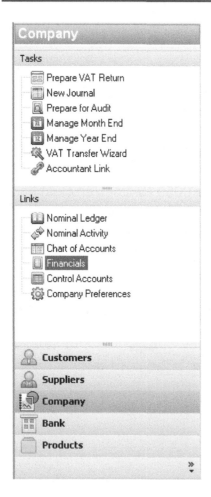

Step One: From the **Company** screen, select "**Financials**" in the links section.

This will create a new screen, from which you can quickly produce a series of the most useful reports in Sage, including the Trial Balance, the Balance Sheet and the Profit and Loss Account.

Step Two: Double-click on 'Financials' to show this screen.

Step Three: From the toolbar at the top of the Financials screen:

Select the  Trial icon.

Step Four: You are now asked to select how you want to view the report.

KAPLAN PUBLISHING

For now, you will just preview the report (i.e. view it on screen). Highlight this and the press the [Run] button.

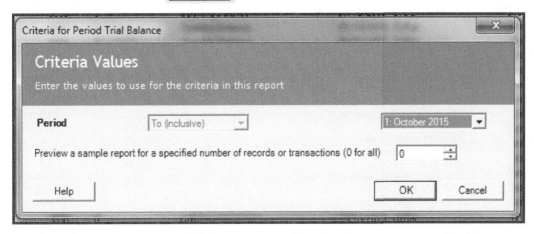

You want to view the trial balance as at October 2015, to see all of the opening balances you have entered. Make sure you amend the date box to October 2015. Leave the next box as 0, and click [OK]

This should bring up a trial balance showing balances for the period up to October 2015. You may need to maximise the screen to see the whole report on screen – do this by clicking the *maximise* icon in the top right corner of the window ([□])

If you have entered everything correctly you should see that both columns (debit and credit) balance to £81,213.28 and there should be no account called 'Suspense' in the list.

You should now print out this trial balance and keep it safe.

| Date: | 31/08/2016 | | TotalPhoto Ltd. | | Page: | 1 |
| Time: | 22:44:58 | | **Period Trial Balance** | | | |

To Period: Month 1, October 2015

N/C	Name	Debit	Credit
0030	Office Equipment	4,849.00	
0031	Office Equipment Depreciation		921.00
0032	Photographic Equipment	22,718.00	
0033	Photographic Equipment Depreciation		4,316.00
0050	Motor Vehicles	21,800.00	
0051	Motor Vehicles Depreciation		5,450.00
1001	Stock	7,403.00	
1100	Debtors Control Account	4,053.10	
1200	Bank Current Account	10,293.00	
1230	Petty Cash	250.00	
2100	Creditors Control Account		19,192.41
2202	VAT Liability		1,623.29
3000	Capital - Ordinary Shares		20,000.00
3200	Retained Profits		5,498.28
4000	Sales - Individuals & Families		5,401.21
4001	Sales - Weddings		3,984.50
4002	Sales - Corporate		1,932.09
4003	Sales - Nurseries and Schools		11,304.20
4004	Other Sales		1,590.30
5000	Purchases - Film	205.63	
5001	Purchases - Paper	1,034.35	
5002	Purchases - Cartridges and Toner	1,225.87	
5003	Purchases - Stationery	409.35	
5004	Purchases - Other Consumables	823.52	
6900	Miscellaneous Expenses	229.39	
7100	Rent	3,800.00	
7103	Rates	480.00	
7304	Motor Expenses	1,035.64	
7502	Telephone	603.43	
	Totals:	81,213.28	81,213.28

This shows what your trial balance should look like after entering all of the opening balances.

If you have managed to follow this manual so far, and produce a trial balance to match the above – well done! You are now ready to move on.

How to amend an incorrect opening balance

If any of the balances are different to the ones on your printed version, you are able to amend as follows:

Firstly tick off your trial balance to determine which opening balances have been entered incorrectly and make a note of them.

Go to the '**Company**' screen and find the first incorrect nominal ledger account in the list and double click on it.

Then click on '**OB**'.

You will then need to decide what it is required to amend the incorrect balance. For example if you had entered the bank current account as £12,293.00 Dr as opposed to the correct balance of £10293.00 Dr, you would need to credit the account with £2000.00 to reduce it to the correct figure. If you prefer, you can reverse your original entry by doing the exact opposite of what you did originally. In the example error above, enter an opening balance of £12,293.00 Cr and that will revert the account back to its original nil balance. You can then repeat the step with the correct figure.

After you have amended and saved any incorrect balances you can print off another Trial Balance to check that it is correct.

Entering transactions

ASSESSMENT CRITERIA
Process sales invoices and credit notes (2.1)
Allocate receipts from customers (2.2)
Process purchase invoices and credit notes (2.3)
Allocate payments to suppliers (2.4)
Process receipts and payments for non-credit transactions (3.1)
Process petty cash receipts and payments (3.3)
Produce routine reports for customers and suppliers (5.1)
Produce routine reports from the general ledger (5.2)

CONTENTS

1 Introduction

Any business will carry out a wide range of transactions every day of the week. However, the majority of these will fall into one of the following categories:

Credit transactions

- Purchases of inventory/stock on credit
- Sales of goods or services on credit

Cash transactions

- Purchases made by cash/cheque/card
- Sales made for cash/cheque/card
- Payments made to suppliers (for goods/services bought on credit)
- Receipts from customers (for goods/services sold on credit)
- Payments made to meet other expenses
- Payment of salaries and wages to staff
- Petty cash transactions
- Transactions directly through the bank account (e.g. bank charges, interest, direct debits, standing orders)

Each of these transactions will have an effect on two accounts within the Sage system – this is the underlying principle of double-entry bookkeeping. However, Sage simplifies this by carrying out much of the double entry automatically.

Consider firstly the first transactions – purchases and sales made on credit. This means that a legally binding contract is established between the two parties, and (usually) the goods or services are supplied but payment is not paid until some later date. The key document in this process is the **invoice** – as this is the document which demands payment and lays down the agreed terms of the transaction.

Hence, entering a credit transaction (whether a purchase or a sale) is a two stage process in Sage:

1   Enter the details of the invoice against the relevant supplier or customer. This will establish the presence and value of the legally binding debt.

2   At a later date, enter the details of the payment of the debt, either the payment sent to the supplier or the receipt received from the customer.

Note that this approach is applicable for both credit sales and credit purchases – you just have to be sure to enter the details in the correct part of Sage.

Now consider the second transactions – each of these has a direct impact on the bank accounts within Sage.

2   Credit sales – entering customer invoices

Our case study company TotalPhoto Ltd have had a number of credit customers by 30th September. Each of these have been issued with an invoice, but these invoices now need to be entered into Sage.

The easiest way to do this is to **batch** invoices together so that they can be input at the same time.

To enter a batch of customer (sales) invoices go to the '**CUSTOMERS'** module and then press the '**INVOICE'** button.

You can then insert data into the next screen as follows:

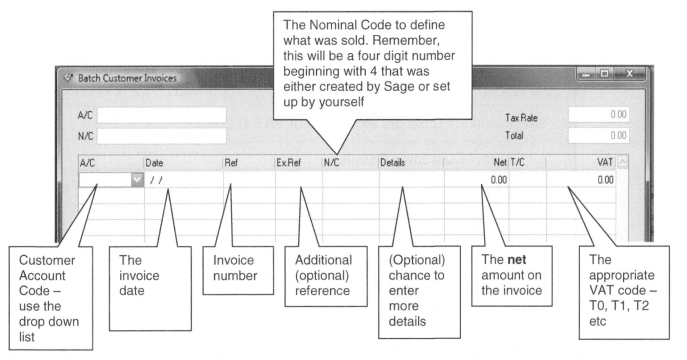

Once you have entered all invoices in the batch you should then review them to ensure you have entered them correctly, and then [Save] them. This will post the invoices to Sage and update the system accordingly.

Activity

Enter the following six invoices for TotalPhoto Ltd using the batch invoicing method. Note that you will also have to create new customer accounts in some cases. **It is advisable to do this before you start entering details of the invoices.**

Date	Invoice No	A/c No	Customer	Nominal Code	Net Amount
30/09/2016	1	POP002	Poppy	4000	£105.00
30/09/2016	2	HAS004	Haslam	4000	£24.50
30/09/2016	3	PAR006	Pargenter	4000	£12.00
30/09/2016	4	SMI009	Smith *(see below)*	4001	£600.00
30/09/2016	5	LUL002	Lullabies Nursery	4003	£100.00
30/09/2016	6	CAM004	Campbell & Dunn	4002	£45.00
30/09/2016	7	HAS004	Haslam	4000	£12.00

All amounts in the table are **exclusive** of VAT at 20%

> **New Customer Details**
>
> Mr A Smith
> 12 Main Street
> Miltonby
> Lancashire
> LN87 4DF
>
> A/c Ref SMI009
>
> Credit terms: Payment in 14 days
>
> Credit Limit: £1000.00

Enter the details in the batch customer invoices screen as detailed below. You can choose suitable wording for the 'details' tab and a suggestion has been given for each.

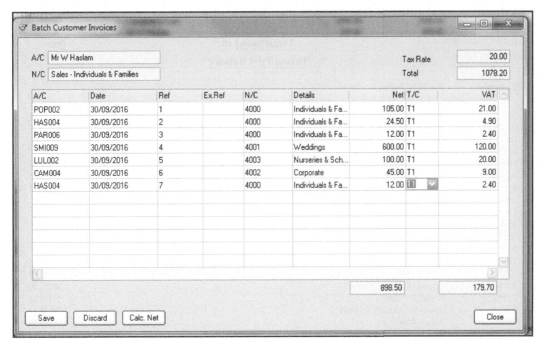

When you have entered all seven invoices, your screen should look like this. Check for accuracy, and when you are happy press the  button.

📝 Activity

Print out another trial balance for September 2016. Compare the two reports and identify the changes that have occurred.

Here is a copy of how the Trial Balance should look.

Date: 28/08/2016 Time: 12:50:48	TotalPhoto Ltd. Period Trial Balance	Page: 1	

To Period: Month 12, September 2016

N/C	Name	Debit	Credit
0030	Office Equipment	4,849.00	
0031	Office Equipment Depreciation		921.00
0032	Photographic Equipment	22,718.00	
0033	Photographic Equipment Depreciation		4,316.00
0050	Motor Vehicles	21,800.00	
0051	Motor Vehicles Depreciation		5,450.00
1001	Stock	7,403.00	
1100	Debtors Control Account	5,131.30	
1200	Bank Current Account	10,293.00	
1230	Petty Cash	250.00	
2100	Creditors Control Account		19,192.41
2200	Sales Tax Control Account		179.70
2202	VAT Liability		1,623.29
3000	Capital - Ordinary Shares		20,000.00
3200	Retained Profits		5,498.28
4000	Sales - Individuals & Families		5,554.71
4001	Sales - Weddings		4,584.50
4002	Sales - Corporate		1,977.09
4003	Sales - Nurseries and Schools		11,404.20
4004	Other Sales		1,590.30
5000	Purchases - Film	205.63	
5001	Purchases - Paper	1,034.35	
5002	Purchases - Cartridges and Toner	1,225.87	
5003	Purchases - Stationery	409.35	
5004	Purchases - Other Consumables	823.52	
6900	Miscellaneous Expenses	229.39	
7100	Rent	3,800.00	
7103	Rates	480.00	
7304	Motor Expenses	1,035.64	
7502	Telephone	603.43	
	Totals:	82,291.48	82,291.48

Notice which figures have changed

(1)   N/C 1100 (Debtors control account) has increased from £4053.10 to £5131.30. This reflects the fact that TotalPhoto Ltd is now owed an additional £1078.20 by its debtors/receivables.

(2)   N/Cs 4000, 4001, 4002 and 4003 have increased, representing the new sales that the company made on 30th September. Note that the increase in these figures (£898.50) is the **net** increase in sales.

(3)   There is a new Nominal Code (2200) called 'Sales Tax Control Account'. This control account automatically records all input VAT (on purchases) and output VAT (on sales) and is used to calculate and produce the company's VAT Return. The amount on this code is currently £179.70 (a **credit** balance) – the VAT charged on all the sales invoices you have entered.

If you would like to see the 'movement' in more detail, i.e. viewing how the balances have changed from the opening balances positions until now – try running the Nominal Activity Report for the same period of time, for the selected accounts.

Firstly, click on the 'Company' module and then select 'Reports' from the menu at the top of the screen:

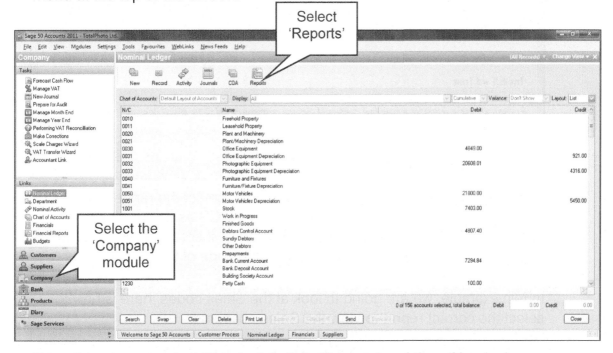

From this screen, select 'Nominal Activity Reports' and then 'Nominal Activity' as shown below:

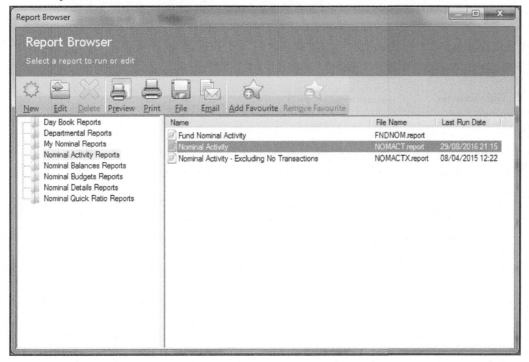

This screen will then appear:

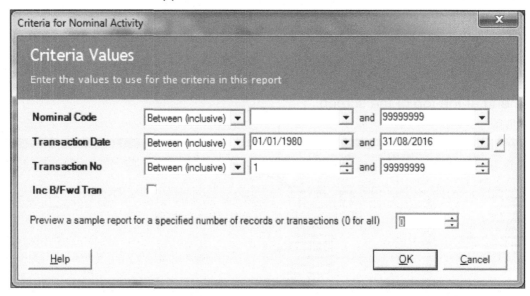

You can use the 'Nominal Code' drop down to select the range of codes you would like the report to generate. In the UACS assessment you may be required to simply print one or two accounts, if so, you can select 'Is' from the drop down menu and then enter the code of the account you would like to view.

In this example, we are going to look at the Sales codes, here is how to select the correct report to view the Sales accounts:

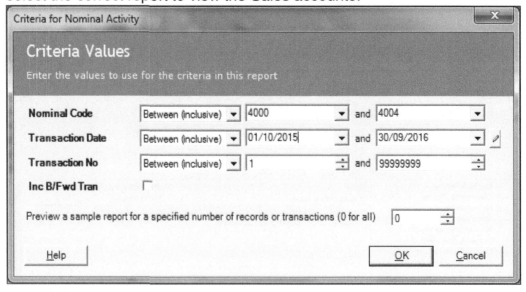

Date:	31/08/2016				**TotalPhoto Ltd.**					Page:	1
Time:	23:15:10				**Nominal Activity**						

Date From:	01/01/1980			N/C From:	4000
Date To:	30/09/2016			N/C To:	4004

Transaction From:	1
Transaction To:	73

N/C:	4000	Name:	Sales - Individuals & Families	Account Balance:	5,554.71 CR

No	Type	Date	Account	Ref	Details	Dept	T/C	Value	Debit	Credit	V	B
43	JC	01/10/2015	4000	O/Bal	Opening Balance	0	T9	5,401.21		5,401.21	-	-
67	SI	30/09/2016	POP002	1	Individuals & Families	0	T1	105.00		105.00	N	-
68	SI	30/09/2016	HAS004	2	Individuals & Families	0	T1	24.50		24.50	N	-
69	SI	30/09/2016	PAR006	3	Individuals & Families	0	T1	12.00		12.00	N	-
73	SI	30/09/2016	HAS004	7	Individuals & Families	0	T1	12.00		12.00	N	-
							Totals:			5,554.71		
							History Balance:			5,554.71		

N/C:	4001	Name:	Sales - Weddings	Account Balance:	4,584.50 CR

No	Type	Date	Account	Ref	Details	Dept	T/C	Value	Debit	Credit	V	B
45	JC	01/10/2015	4001	O/Bal	Opening Balance	0	T9	3,984.50		3,984.50	-	-
70	SI	30/09/2016	SMI009	4	Weddings	0	T1	600.00		600.00	N	-
							Totals:			4,584.50		
							History Balance:			4,584.50		

N/C:	4002	Name:	Sales - Corporate	Account Balance:	1,977.09 CR

No	Type	Date	Account	Ref	Details	Dept	T/C	Value	Debit	Credit	V	B
47	JC	01/10/2015	4002	O/Bal	Opening Balance	0	T9	1,932.09		1,932.09	-	-
72	SI	30/09/2016	CAM004	6	Corporate	0	T1	45.00		45.00	N	-
							Totals:			1,977.09		
							History Balance:			1,977.09		

N/C:	4003	Name:	Sales - Nurseries and Schools	Account Balance:	11,404.20 CR

No	Type	Date	Account	Ref	Details	Dept	T/C	Value	Debit	Credit	V	B
49	JC	01/10/2015	4003	O/Bal	Opening Balance	0	T9	11,304.20		11,304.20	-	-
71	SI	30/09/2016	LUL002	5	Nurseries & Schools	0	T1	100.00		100.00	N	-
							Totals:			11,404.20		
							History Balance:			11,404.20		

N/C:	4004	Name:	Other Sales	Account Balance:	1,590.30 CR

No	Type	Date	Account	Ref	Details	Dept	T/C	Value	Debit	Credit	V	B
51	JC	01/10/2015	4004	O/Bal	Opening Balance	0	T9	1,590.30		1,590.30	-	-
							Totals:			1,590.30		
							History Balance:			1,590.30		

3 Customer credit notes

A credit note is essentially a 'negative invoice' and is produced and sent to customers when a refund is needed. The most likely time this will happen is when goods that the organisation has sold to a customer have been returned as faulty. However, they can also be used to correct errors.

Producing a credit note in Sage is straightforward and effectively mirrors the process for producing an invoice.

Activity

Let us suppose that the sale of a 6" × 4" colour print made by TotalPhoto Ltd to Miss Pargenter for £12.00 (plus VAT) (Invoice No 3) is returned as faulty. It is necessary to issue a credit note so that this debt is effectively 'removed' from Miss Pargenter's account. Enter the credit note on Sage and guidance on how to enter follows.

How to process a customer credit note

From the **CUSTOMER** module select **CUSTOMER LIST** and then from the

icons at the top of the screen select the icon.

Here you can enter a batch of Credit Notes (just as you did with the batched invoices). **Sage shows your entries in RED to make it obvious that this is a Credit Note.**

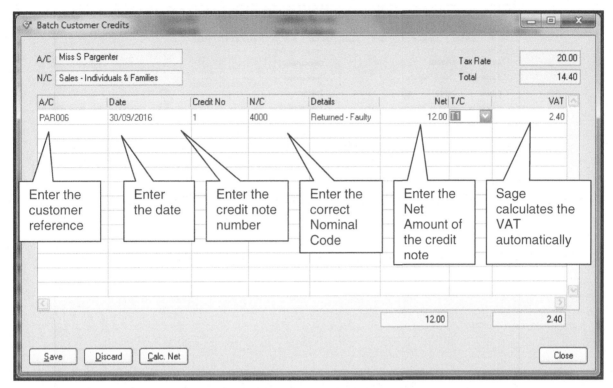

When you have entered all Credit Note(s) in the batch, and checked their accuracy, **SAVE** them to ensure that Sage can process them.

Viewing a customer's account

From the Customer List, locate 'Miss S Pargenter' by visually scanning down the list and double-clicking on the line.

This will take you to the record of 'Miss S Pargenter'.

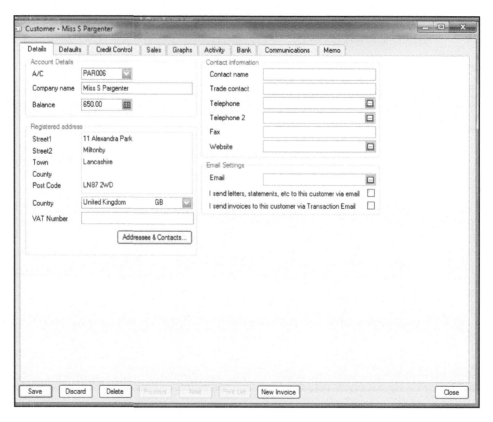

You want to view the activity to this account so once in the record, click on the activity tab at the top of the page:

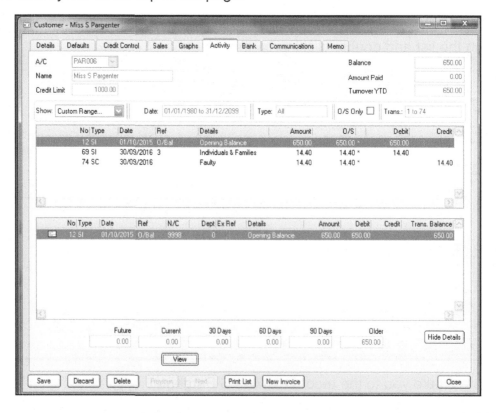

In the 'Show' drop down menu, select 'this financial year. This will then display all of the activity that has taken place in this account between 1st October 2015 and 30th September 2016. Additional filters around transaction types and status can also be used to refine the view.

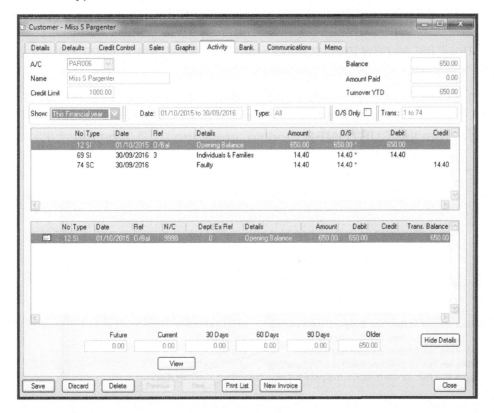

You will be able to see the opening balance and the invoices and credit note already posted. Other transactions that could appear here include, payments received and refunds made – these will be covered later on in this text.

All transactions on a customer account have their original values plus a balance i.e. the amount of the transaction that has not been paid or refunded.

4 Producing customer statements

Having produced and sent invoices to customers, most businesses will also need to send periodic (usually monthly) statements to their customers which will list all new transactions – such as their new purchases, payments sent, credit notes issued to them etc.

Sage allows the easy creation and production of customer statements.

Firstly, from the **CUSTOMER** module, press the  button.

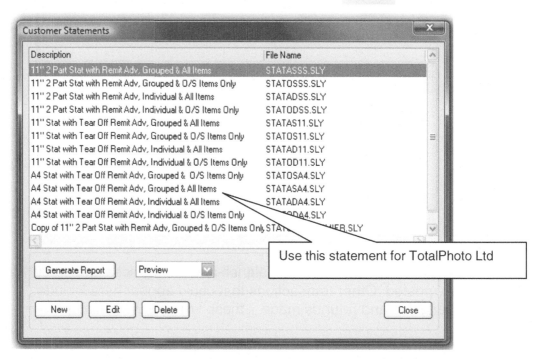

This provides a choice of different statement layouts. You should use the one which best suits your business needs. However, for the purposes of this manual you should use the one called 'A4 Stat with Tear off Remit. Adv. Grouped & All Items'. Select this one by double-clicking.

In the **CRITERIA** screen (see below) use the pull-down menus to select customer Haslam (Ref HAS004). You can use the 'From...to...' feature to select a range of customers – but for now just select this one.

Make sure to enter the required transaction dates. The examples below use '01/10/2015' to '30/09/2016' for the transaction dates as they relate to the dates used in the case study for TotalPhoto Ltd.

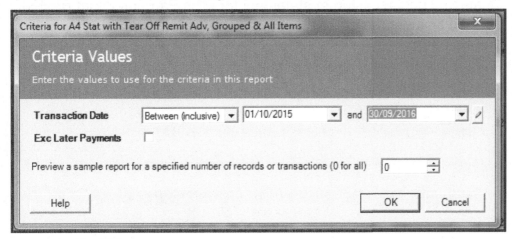

Press [OK] to create the report.

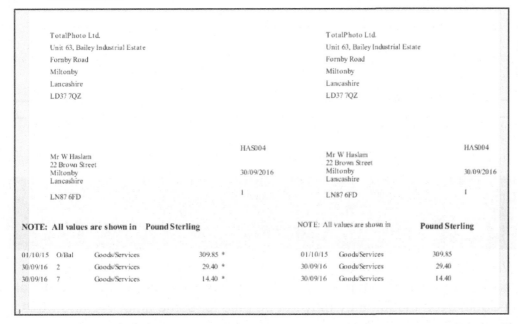

This statement could then be printed out (using special stationery if required) and then sent to customers.

Activity

Create and print a customer statement for Miss Pargenter (Ref PAR006)
It should look like this:

TotalPhoto Ltd.				TotalPhoto Ltd.		
Unit 63, Bailey Industrial Estate				Unit 63, Bailey Industrial Estate		
Fornby Road				Fornby Road		
Miltonby				Miltonby		
Lancashire				Lancashire		
LD37 7QZ				LD37 7QZ		

	PAR006			PAR006
Miss S Pargenter		Miss S Pargenter	
11 Alexandra Park		11 Alexandra Park	
Miltonby	30/09/2016	Miltonby	30/09/2016
Lancashire		Lancashire	
LN87 2WD	1	LN87 2WD	1

NOTE: All values are shown in Pound Sterling   NOTE: All values are shown in **Pound Sterling**

01/10/15	O/Bal	Goods/Services	650.00 *		01/10/15	Goods/Services	650.00	
30/09/16	3	Goods/Services	14.40 *		30/09/16	Goods/Services	14.40	
30/09/16		Credit	*	14.40	30/09/16	Credit		14.40

5 Credit purchases – entering supplier invoices

When an organisation purchases goods or services on credit, it will receive an invoice from the supplier. These must be recorded immediately in Sage, even though they may not be paid for some time. We know this is when the business has purchased on credit, i.e. to pay later.

The most common way to process supplier invoices is to **batch** them (in much the same way as you did with the invoices to customers). This way, a number of invoices can be processed at the same time.

The process for entering batches of supplier statements is very similar to that for entering batches of customer invoices – except it is accessed via the **SUPPLIERS** module.

You should enter the **SUPPLIERS** module now.

Press the icon and enter the invoice details required.

Activity

TotalPhoto Ltd received the following five invoices on 30th September 2016.

Invoice Ref	Supplier	Account	Net amount	Nominal Code
1341	Mackay Films	MF001	£208.76	5000
209	The Stationery Cupboard	SC003	£14.65	5003
216	The Stationery Cupboard	SC003	£78.92	5003
2203	Octopus Inks Ltd	OI001	£309.28	5002
10092	Mills Paper Products	MP002	£162.52	5001

You should now enter the above five supplier invoices as a batch. You can choose suitable wording for the 'details' tab and a suggestion has been given for each.

When you have done the above activity the screen should look like this:

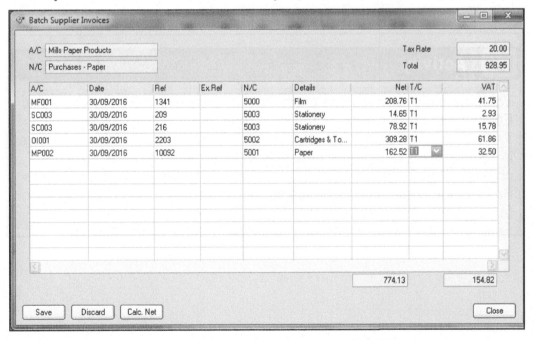

You should verify the entries and then press the '**SAVE**' button to post your entries to Sage.

6 Supplier credit notes

These are processed in exactly the same way as you processed credit notes issued to customers.

Access the entry screen from the **SUPPLIERS** module.

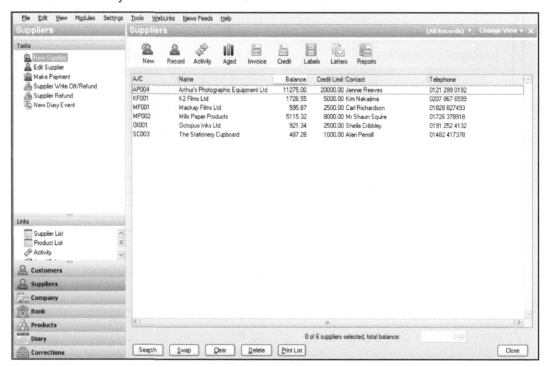

 Activity

TotalPhoto Ltd receives one credit note. It is from Arthur's Photographic Equipment Ltd (Ref AP004) and is a credit for £2,109.99 (excluding VAT) for a camera that was returned as faulty. The credit note reference is 134C and the date of the transaction is 30th September 2016. The nominal code for this is 0032 (Fixed Asset – Photographic Equipment). Process the credit note using a suitable narrative for the details section (a suggestion has been shown).

Your entry screen for the above activity should look like this:

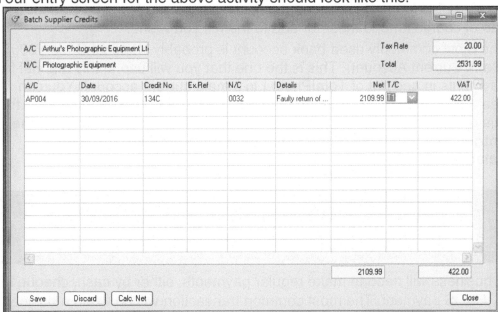

Again – note that Sage shows your entries in red so that they are easily identifiable as a credit note. When you have checked the accuracy of your entries you should press the '**SAVE**' button.

7 Bank transactions

Sage allows you to run a number of 'bank accounts'. These need not necessarily all be held at a bank – they could also include cash in hand, petty cash etc.

The principles for making payments in or out of any of these accounts are the same.

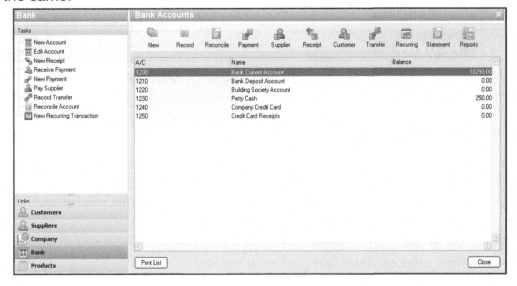

Enter the **Bank** module. You can see that Sage has already set up a number of different bank accounts, each with its own Nominal Code. You can of course amend these or add to them if you wish.

The most commonly used bank account is probably Nominal Code 1200 (Bank Current Account). This is the one that you will use in this manual for payments in and out of TotalPhoto Ltd's main current account. You can see that it has a balance at the moment of £10,293.00. You may recall that this relates to the opening balance that you entered earlier. **None of the entries that you have made since then have affected the bank balance**.

8   Making payments by BACS and cheque

A business will need to make regular payments, either by cash, cheque or by BACS payment. The most common transaction will be when a business pays its suppliers when they have previously bought on credit (promised to pay later). However, they may simply need to pay for day to day expenses. We can now look at the process of entering these types of payments in Sage.

9   Remittance advices

It is common for businesses to produce a remittance advice when raising payments to suppliers. This document would notify the supplier of any invoices that are being paid, and also any credit notes which have been incorporated in to the payment. It is a simple exercise to raise a remittance advice and guidance follows.

Activity

TotalPhoto Ltd has three payments to make on 30th September 2016. These are:

- A cheque for £107.65 plus VAT at 20% to Arrow Telecoms to pay the telephone bill
- A cheque for £55.00 to Miltonby Cricket Association for advertising in their League Handbook (this transaction is exempt from VAT)
- A cheque for £45.00 to Miltonby Borough Council for a parking permit (this transaction attracts zero rated VAT)

Enter the above transactions on to Sage and raise the relevant remittance advices. Detailed guidance follows.

Click the button within the 'Bank' screen.

Enter each transaction as a separate line. Be careful to make sure you select the appropriate Nominal Code for the expense item, and also the correct VAT rate. Your entries should look like this:

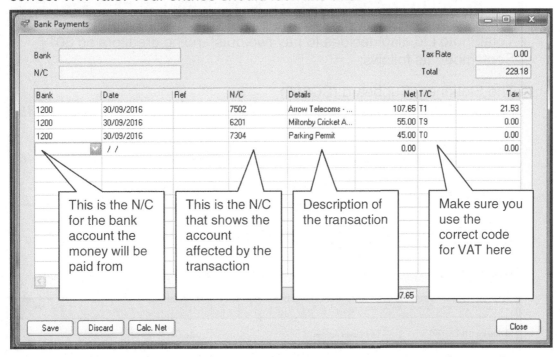

You could also include extra optional details such as the cheque number or BACS in the '**Ref**' box. When you have checked your entries, **SAVE** them to Sage.

Now check the balance on Nominal Code 1200 (the bank current account).

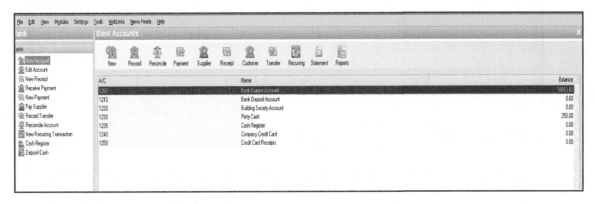

See how the bank balance has now gone down to **£10063.82** – reflecting the fact that payments of £229.18 (£207.65 plus £21.53 VAT) have been taken from it.

Paying suppliers

We can now look at the other common area for payments which is paying suppliers when the business has previously bought goods on credit. This is especially common for buying inventory/stock.

Activity

TotalPhoto Ltd also decides to pay two outstanding creditors on 30th September, as follows:

The Stationery Cupboard (SC003)
Amount: £375 inc VAT   *Paid by cheque number 00245*

K2 Films Ltd (KF001)
Amount £1726.55 (inc VAT).   *Paid by cheque number 00246*

Enter these supplier payments onto Sage. Guidance follows.

To enter these payments onto Sage click the 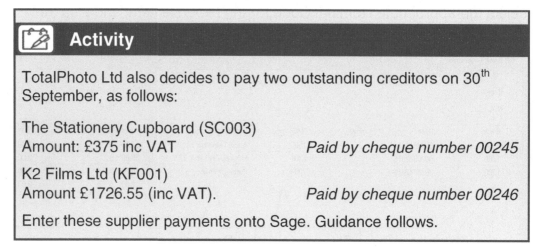 button within the Bank module.

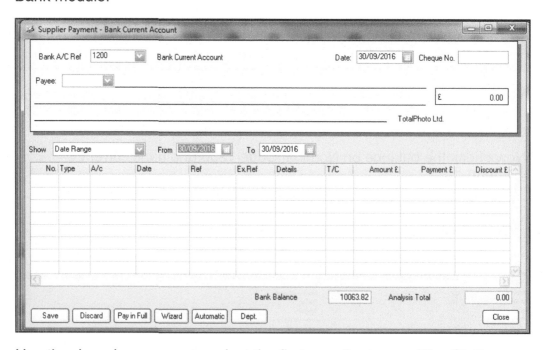

Use the drop down menu to select the first supplier to pay (The Stationery Cupboard). Enter the correct date, the cheque number or 'BACS' in the 'Cheque No' box, and the amount being paid (£375.00). In this case the amount has been paid by cheque.

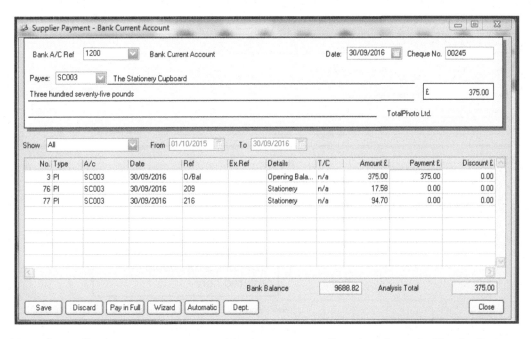

Note how Sage presents you with the outstanding invoices in the bottom half of the screen for the particular supplier. This allows you to decide which outstanding invoices you want to pay.

Enter £375.00 against the opening balance amount – this is the invoice being paid on this occasion.

Note that Sage can automatically decide which invoices to pay, or, if you wish to pay **all** outstanding invoices, you can select to Pay in Full

It is important in the assessment that you allocate supplier payments correctly. In this example we have paid the full amount of the opening balance and therefore to allocate this accurately it is important that it is entered against the opening balance line.

You may also be asked to make a part payment of an opening balance/invoice, in which case you would simply type the amount in next the payment box, next to the balance that you are part paying. Alternatively, you may be asked to post an amount as 'a payment on account' in which case you simply type the amount in the box at the top of the screen.

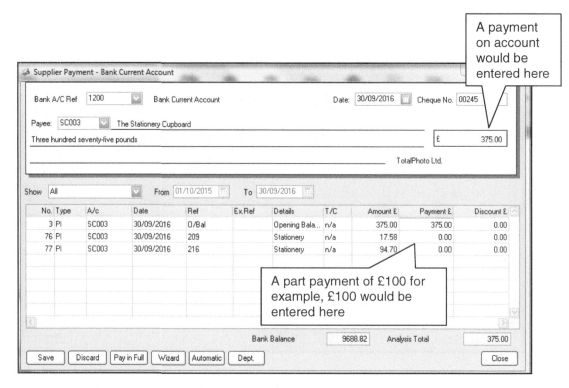

Important!

Before you click save, click the **'Create Remittance'** icon to generate the remittance advice. The best option to choose is A4 size and you can choose to display in preview format or print direct to the printer. Click '**Run**' to generate the report. Once you have raised the report you can click '**Save**' to generate the payment. It should look like this depending on the format you have chosen.

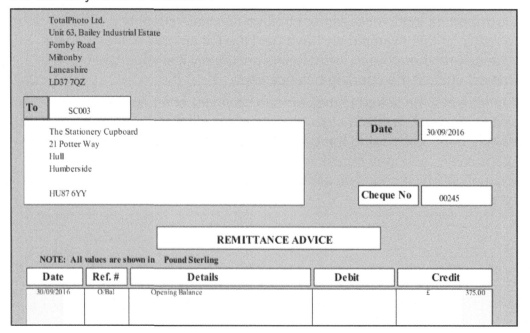

Now enter the next payment to K2 Films Ltd, in the same way.

10 Recording receipts by BACS and cheque

The most likely sources of receipts for most businesses are:

- Cash sales
- Receipts from Debtors/Receivables which are customers who have previously bought goods on credit.

We will look at these in turn.

Cash sales

These are transactions that relate to sales made for cash rather than on credit. The funds are received immediately by the business in the form of cash, cheque or card.

 Activity

TotalPhoto Ltd also sells items to two customers who pay cash on 30th September. The first of these is a 6" × 4" Colour Print for £12.00 plus VAT (use nominal code 4000); the second is for School Photos (Set 2) for £28.00 plus VAT of 20% (nominal code 4003).

Enter these cash sales into the bank current account on Sage. Detailed guidance follows.

Click the button within the 'Bank' screen.

Enter each transaction on a separate line. Be careful to make sure you select the appropriate nominal code for the sales, and also the correct VAT rate. Your entries should look like this:

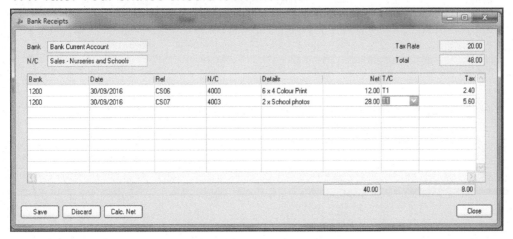

Click the **SAVE** button to post your entries to Sage.

11 Receipts from customers

Businesses will regularly receive cheques and BACS receipts from customers that have previously bought from them on credit.

 Activity

On 30th September TotalPhoto Ltd also received two amounts from customers in respect of their outstanding invoices. These were:

Lullabies Nursery (LUL002)   Cheque for £726.90

Mrs H Poppy   Cash £120.00

Enter these transactions onto Sage. Guidance follows.

To enter these, firstly click the icon from with the **Bank** module.

Then enter the details of the first payment as follows.

Click **Save** to post this entry to Sage.

> Be sure to use the correct Bank Account

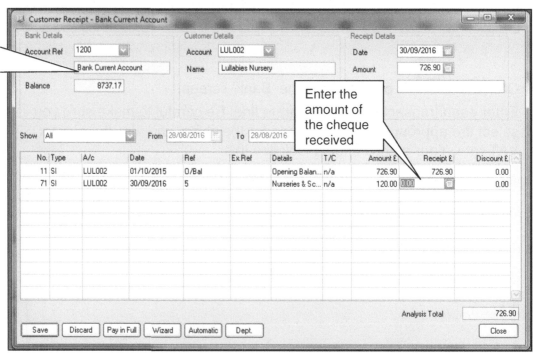

KAPLAN PUBLISHING

Now enter the second receipt, from Mrs Poppy. Note that only £120.00 has been received, and that she paid in cash. This amount does not match any particular invoice, so unless notified otherwise allocate this against the oldest debt. Instead of being able to click 'pay in full' you will need to enter the amount manually in the receipt box. Your screen should look like this:

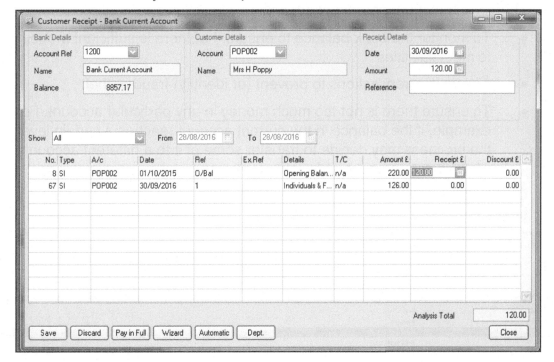

Again, click on **Save.**

BACS receipts

When recording BACS receipts, you should follow the same process as when you record a cheque receipt from a customer. However, instead of entering the cheque number in the reference box, you will need to enter 'BACS' instead. The date entered should match the date that the BACS has appeared on the bank statement or the date given on the accompanying remittance advice sent by the customer.

12 Checking bank activity

It is important for businesses to regularly check their bank transactions. There are a number of reasons for this:

- To monitor the bank balance to ensure that there is sufficient money to meet liabilities

- To monitor transactions to prevent (or identify) fraud or theft

- To ensure there is not too much money in any particular account. For example, if the balance in the current account reaches a certain level the business may decide to transfer some of it to a different account where it may earn a higher rate of interest.

Checking the activity on any Nominal Code (**not just for the bank**) is straightforward.

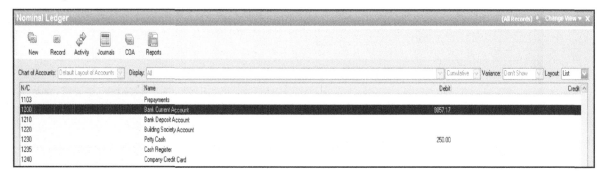

Highlight the account (within the Company screen) you want to check, and then double-click on it with the mouse.

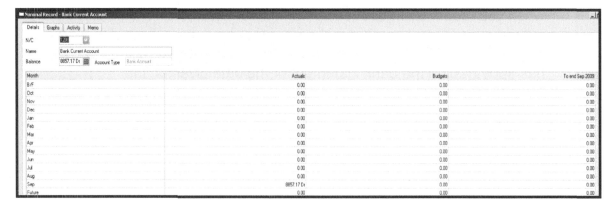

Choose the Activity tab at the top.

KAPLAN PUBLISHING

You should now see the following screen:

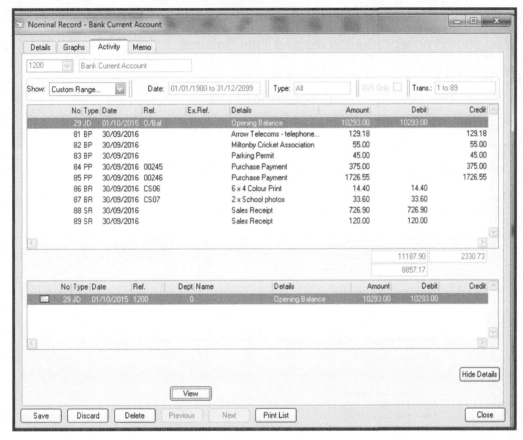

This shows all the transactions to date affecting N/C 1200 (the main current account). Make sure you can identify all of these.

Note that Debit entries represent monies paid **into** the bank account; credit entries show payments **out of** the bank account.

Activity

You should now produce a revised Trial Balance.

Your Trial Balance should now look like this.

TotalPhoto Ltd

Period Trial Balance

Date:	28/08/2016		TotalPhoto Ltd.		Page:	1
Time:	14:36:26		Period Trial Balance			

To Period: Month 12, September 2016

N/C	Name	Debit	Credit
0030	Office Equipment	4,849.00	
0031	Office Equipment Depreciation		921.00
0032	Photographic Equipment	20,608.01	
0033	Photographic Equipment Depreciation		4,316.00
0050	Motor Vehicles	21,800.00	
0051	Motor Vehicles Depreciation		5,450.00
1001	Stock	7,403.00	
1100	Debtors Control Account	4,270.00	
1200	Bank Current Account	8,857.17	
1230	Petty Cash	250.00	
2100	Creditors Control Account		15,487.82
2200	Sales Tax Control Account		185.30
2201	Purchase Tax Control Account		245.65
2202	VAT Liability		1,623.29
3000	Capital - Ordinary Shares		20,000.00
3200	Retained Profits		5,498.28
4000	Sales - Individuals & Families		5,554.71
4001	Sales - Weddings		4,584.50
4002	Sales - Corporate		1,977.09
4003	Sales - Nurseries and Schools		11,432.20
4004	Other Sales		1,590.30
5000	Purchases - Film	414.39	
5001	Purchases - Paper	1,196.87	
5002	Purchases - Cartridges and Toner	1,535.15	
5003	Purchases - Stationery	502.92	
5004	Purchases - Other Consumables	823.52	
6201	Advertising	55.00	
6900	Miscellaneous Expenses	229.39	
7100	Rent	3,800.00	
7103	Rates	480.00	
7304	Motor Expenses	1,080.64	
7502	Telephone	711.08	
	Totals:	78,866.14	78,866.14

13 Transfers

Sometimes a business may transfer money from one account to another. For example, it may transfer money from 'Petty Cash' to the 'Bank Current Account' or vice versa. Alternatively, it may transfer an amount from the current account to a deposit account.

Activity

TotalPhoto Ltd currently have £250.00 in their petty cash tin and think this is too much. Therefore, they want to transfer £150.00 from the petty cash account to the bank current account. They take £150 out of the tin, then take it to the bank and pay it into the bank current account.

Process this transaction onto SAGE. Guidance follows.

From the **Bank** module click the 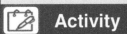 icon.

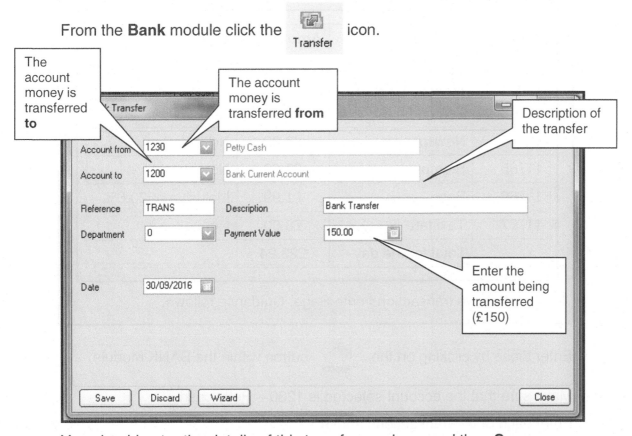

You should enter the details of this transfer as above and then **Save**.

14 Petty cash

Most businesses use petty cash as a way of paying for minor expenses such as taxi fares, tea, milk and coffee, window cleaning etc.

Payments out of petty cash are recorded in exactly the same way as any other payments made from a bank account. Remember to make sure that you use the correct account number (1230).

Also be sure to enter the correct VAT code for each transaction. Many items commonly paid for out of petty cash are zero-rated or exempt – but not all.

 Activity

TotalPhoto Ltd makes the following payments out of petty cash on 30th September 2016

Voucher No	Description	Amount	VAT?
11762	Window cleaner	£4.00	No
11763	Tea and milk	£2.65	No
11764	Newspapers	£3.00	No
11765	Stamps	£3.60	No
11766	Pens	£1.99	Inclusive at 20.0%
11767	Taxi fare	£8.00	No
	Total for the day	£23.24	

Enter the above transactions onto Sage. Guidance follows.

Enter these by clicking on the button within the BANK module.

Make sure that the account selected is 1230 – Petty cash.

Enter each of the transactions above.

Your screen should look like this:

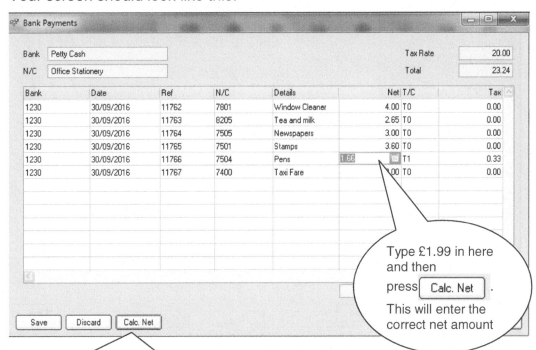

If you have a VAT-inclusive amount, Sage will automatically calculate the VAT element for you. Simply type the gross amount in the box and press this button, or press F9.

Once you have verified this click **Save.**

Reimbursing the petty cash account

To reimburse the petty cash account, simply transfer the money from one account to the petty cash account.

Activity

TotalPhoto Ltd reimbursed their petty cash tin at the end of 30th September with the amount necessary to bring the float back to £100.00. The amount spent during the day was £23.24 and so this is the amount to be reimbursed. This money was taken from the 'Bank Current Account'

Process the above transaction onto Sage. Guidance follows.

The transfer entry should look like this:

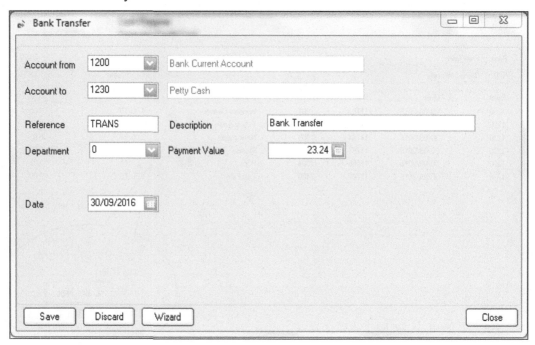

You should now see that the balance on the petty cash account has been restored to £100.00.

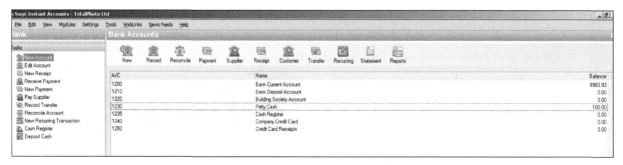

You have now learnt how to process the vast majority of transactions that most businesses will deal with on a day to day basis.

Activity

Print off a trial balance for TotalPhoto Ltd which should look like the one reproduced below.

KAPLAN PUBLISHING

Date:	28/08/2016	TotalPhoto Ltd.		Page:	I
Time:	14:54:25	Period Trial Balance			

To Period: Month 12, September 2016

N/C	Name	Debit	Credit
0030	Office Equipment	4,849.00	
0031	Office Equipment Depreciation		921.00
0032	Photographic Equipment	20,608.01	
0033	Photographic Equipment Depreciation		4,316.00
0050	Motor Vehicles	21,800.00	
0051	Motor Vehicles Depreciation		5,450.00
1001	Stock	7,403.00	
1100	Debtors Control Account	4,270.00	
1200	Bank Current Account	8,983.93	
1230	Petty Cash	100.00	
2100	Creditors Control Account		15,487.82
2200	Sales Tax Control Account		185.30
2201	Purchase Tax Control Account		245.32
2202	VAT Liability		1,623.29
3000	Capital - Ordinary Shares		20,000.00
3200	Retained Profits		5,498.28
4000	Sales - Individuals & Families		5,554.71
4001	Sales - Weddings		4,584.50
4002	Sales - Corporate		1,977.09
4003	Sales - Nurseries and Schools		11,432.20
4004	Other Sales		1,590.30
5000	Purchases - Film	414.39	
5001	Purchases - Paper	1,196.87	
5002	Purchases - Cartridges and Toner	1,535.15	
5003	Purchases - Stationery	502.92	
5004	Purchases - Other Consumables	823.52	
6201	Advertising	55.00	
6900	Miscellaneous Expenses	229.39	
7100	Rent	3,800.00	
7103	Rates	480.00	
7304	Motor Expenses	1,080.64	
7400	Travelling	8.00	
7501	Postage and Carriage	3.60	
7502	Telephone	711.08	
7504	Office Stationery	1.66	
7505	Books etc.	3.00	
7801	Cleaning	4.00	
8205	Refreshments	2.65	
	Totals:	78,865.81	78,865.81

Journals

9

ASSSESSMENT CRITERIA	CONTENTS
Process journals (4.1)	1 Introduction
Produce routine reports from the general ledger (5.2)	2 Correction of errors
	3 Irrecoverable debts

1 Introduction

So far you have learnt how to process day-to-day transactions through Sage. These have included recording sales and purchases and making and receiving payments.

Sometimes, however, a business will need to record an accounting transaction that falls outside the 'norm'. In these instances, a **journal** is required to correct errors or make adjustments.

Common reasons for journals

- Correction of errors – for example, amending opening balances, removing duplicate entries, or correcting errors

- Writing off irrecoverable debts

  Year end adjustments such as depreciation, accruals and prepayments **(you do not need to be aware of these areas for the UACS assessment as they will be covered at a higher level).**

2 Correction of errors

You may find that you enter a transaction incorrectly, and post it to Sage before you have noticed. In certain circumstances you will need to correct the error by producing a reversing journal.

 Activity

Earlier, you entered a payment from the bank for £55.00 to Miltonby Cricket Association for advertising in their handbook.

It has now come to light that the earlier bank payment to Miltonby Cricket Association was incorrect. The payment should have been for £85.00, the error being due to misreading the League Secretary's rather poor handwriting on the invoice. This means that an underpayment of £30.00 has been made in our accounting records. The correct amount was in fact paid – reference to the cheque book stub and the bank statement would confirm this. Use reference JNL001 for this transaction and 'Being the correction of incorrect posting' as the narrative.

Rectify this error in Sage, guidance follows.

The problem

At the moment, the bank balance is overstated by £30, as we have only entered £55 instead of the correct amount of £85. Also, the expenditure on advertising is understated by the same £30.

The solution

You need to produce a journal to correct this error.

From the **Company** module select the 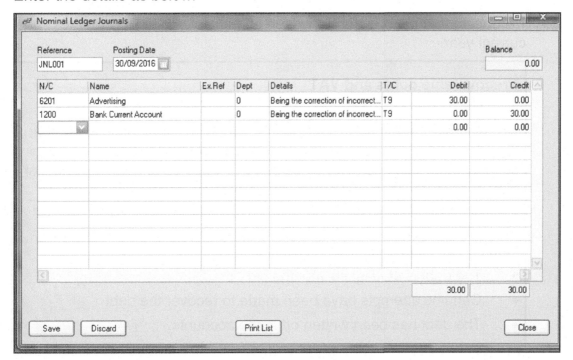 icon.

Enter the details as below:

N/C	Name	Ex.Ref	Dept	Details	T/C	Debit	Credit
6201	Advertising		0	Being the correction of incorrect...	T9	30.00	0.00
1200	Bank Current Account		0	Being the correction of incorrect...	T9	0.00	30.00
						0.00	0.00
						30.00	30.00

Reference: JNL001   **Posting Date:** 30/09/2016   **Balance:** 0.00

Save   Discard   Print List   Close

Note the double-entry:

You have credited the bank account by £30 and debited the advertising account by the same amount.

Press **Save.**

Other methods to deal with corrections

There are alternative ways to deal with correcting errors. For example, the process you covered earlier when an opening balance for a nominal account has been entered incorrectly. There is a later chapter within this textbook which covers 'Corrections' generally.

3 Irrecoverable debts

A bad or irrecoverable debt arises when a customer (debtor/receivable) fails to make payment on their debt. At some point the organisation will need to judge that the debt is no longer likely to be recovered and will need to write off the debt. This has the effect of decreasing the total receivables/debtors (as detailed in the sales ledger control account) and creating an irrecoverable debt expense that will reduce profits.

To write off an irrecoverable debt you will need to perform a 'write off' function for the particular customer for the amount being written off. This will ensure that the bad debt is written off against your profits for the current year.

Irrecoverable debts and VAT

When a customer purchases goods or services on credit, the supplier will generally charge them VAT on that supply (assuming of course that they are VAT registered and the supplies attract VAT). If the customer subsequently fails to pay for these items it would be unfair if the supplier continued to bear the cost of the VAT. Rules exist therefore to protect the supplier in this case.

The VAT can be reclaimed (i.e. offset against a future VAT liability) so long as the following criteria are met:

- The debt is at least six months old
- Genuine attempts have been made to recover the debt
- The debt has been written off in the accounts.

 Activity

TotalPhoto Ltd is currently has as a debtor T Pashby (A/c Ref PAS002). This debt relates to photographs sold almost a year ago. A number of letters have been sent to the given address but have been returned as 'not living at this address anymore'. There have been numerous attempts to contact the customer without any response.

A decision has now been taken to write off the bad debt (£89.50 including VAT). Process this transaction in Sage. Guidance follows.

This is processed as follows:

From within the **CUSTOMERS** module, click on '**CUSTOMER WRITE OFF/REFUND**' as shown here:

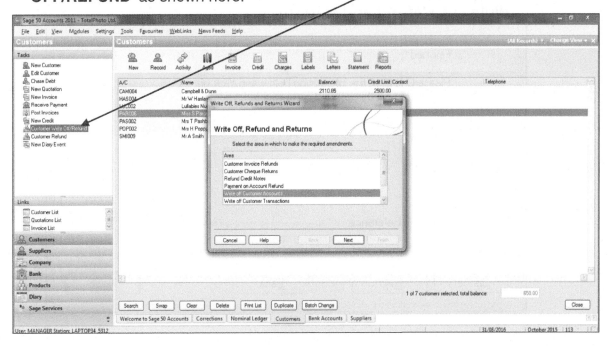

Click on '**Write off Customer Accounts**', then select the customer (Mrs T Pashby). Proceed through the screens, entering 'Irrecoverable debt write off' as the additional reference as below. Check the details are correct before clicking '**Finish**'.

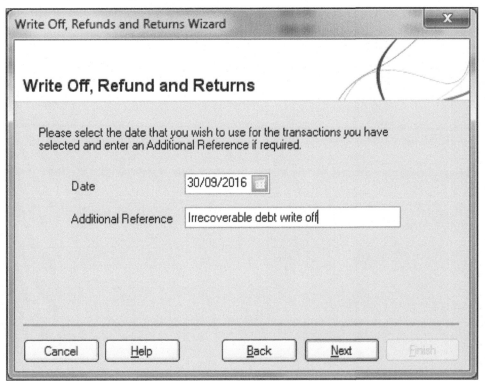

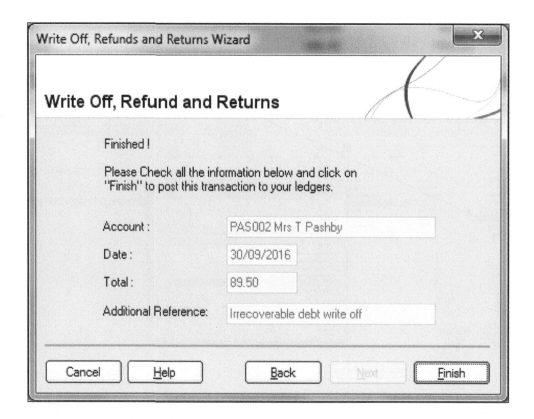

Activity

Run a Trial Balance report for the period 1st October 2015 until 30th September 2016.

Look out for the Bad Debt write off and Advertising accounts, this is how your trial balance should look:

Time:	15:17:21	Period Trial Balance		
To Period:	Month 12, September 2016			
N/C	**Name**		**Debit**	**Credit**
0030	Office Equipment		4,849.00	
0031	Office Equipment Depreciation			921.00
0032	Photographic Equipment		20,608.01	
0033	Photographic Equipment Depreciation			4,316.00
0050	Motor Vehicles		21,800.00	
0051	Motor Vehicles Depreciation			5,450.00
1001	Stock		7,403.00	
1100	Debtors Control Account		4,180.50	
1200	Bank Current Account		8,953.93	
1230	Petty Cash		100.00	
2100	Creditors Control Account			15,487.82
2200	Sales Tax Control Account			185.30
2201	Purchase Tax Control Account			245.32
2202	VAT Liability			1,623.29
3000	Capital - Ordinary Shares			20,000.00
3200	Retained Profits			5,498.28
4000	Sales - Individuals & Families			5,554.71
4001	Sales - Weddings			4,584.50
4002	Sales - Corporate			1,977.09
4003	Sales - Nurseries and Schools			11,432.20
4004	Other Sales			1,590.30
5000	Purchases - Film		414.39	
5001	Purchases - Paper		1,196.87	
5002	Purchases - Cartridges and Toner		1,535.15	
5003	Purchases - Stationery		502.92	
5004	Purchases - Other Consumables		823.52	
6201	Advertising		85.00	
6900	Miscellaneous Expenses		229.39	
7100	Rent		3,800.00	
7103	Rates		480.00	
7304	Motor Expenses		1,080.64	
7400	Travelling		8.00	
7501	Postage and Carriage		3.60	
7502	Telephone		711.08	
7504	Office Stationery		1.66	
7505	Books etc.		3.00	
7801	Cleaning		4.00	
8100	Bad Debt Write Off		89.50	
8205	Refreshments		2.65	
		Totals:	**78,865.81**	**78,865.81**

Advertising costs now show the correct amount of £85.00

The Bad Debt write off account now shows the £89.50 written off from T Pashby

Occasionally, you may be asked to write off a customer account ignoring VAT. Using the wizard will automatically adjust for the VAT.

An alternative way of writing off a bad debt but ignoring VAT would be to raise a credit note on the customer's account but to code the credit note to nominal code 8100 (Bad debts). The following screen shots will show you the process:

We will say for example that Mrs H Poppy has gone into administration and therefore we are unable to recover her debt of £126.00 but this time we will ignore VAT:

Select the Customers module, highlight Mrs H Poppy and click 'Credit' at the top of the screen:

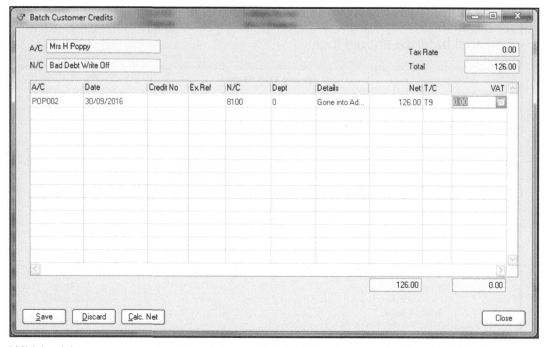

Within this screen, enter the date as 30/09/16, the nominal code 8100 (Bad debt write off) and the net amount of £126.00. As we want to ignore VAT we can enter T9 for the tax code which will ignore the VAT. Once all of the information is correct, click 'Save'.

This is simply an alternative way of writing off a bad debt.

In the UACS assessment, you may be asked to perform the bad debt write off (ignoring VAT). If so, they may ask you to print off the Sales Returns day book.

Bank reconciliation

ASSESSMENT CRITERIA

Reconcile the bank statement (4.2)

Produce routine reports from the general ledger (5.2)

CONTENTS

1 Introduction

A useful exercise for all businesses to undertake on a regular basis is to reconcile their bank account. In essence this means checking the company's own records with the bank statement received from their bank.

We need to review the bank reconciliation process for our case study business. TotalPhoto Ltd received the following statement from their bank.

STATEMENT No 10

5 October 2016

Account number

Sort code

Date		Payments	Receipts	Balance
30/09/16	Op Bal			10293.00C
30/09/16	Counter credit		14.40	10307.40C
30/09/16	Counter credit		33.60	10341.00C
30/09/16	Counter credit		726.90	11067.90C
30/09/16	Counter credit		120.00	11187.90C
30/09/16	Interest		11.22	11199.12C
30/09/16	Bank Charges	31.41		11167.71C
30/09/16	DD North West Radio	240.00		10927.71C
30/09/16	Bank transfer	23.24		10904.47C
30/09/16	Bank transfer		150.00	11054.47C
03/10/16	Chq 242	85.00		10969.47C
03/10/16	Chq 243	129.18		10840.29C
03/10/16	Chq 244	45.00		10795.29C

D = Debit

C = Credit

The bank statement will rarely agree exactly with the company's own records, for three reasons. Let's think about what these are:

1   **Items on the bank statement not yet recorded in Sage**

    There may be some items on the bank statement which do not yet appear in the company's records. Here, there is interest which has been credited to the business' account of £11.22, and also bank charges of £31.41 which have been debited from the account. There is also a direct debit for £240.00. It is likely that the company would not know the exact amount or date of these receipts/payments from the bank account until the statement is actually received. Similarly, you should always check that all standing orders/direct debits/BACS transfers etc have been fully recorded in the company's records. Remember that a 'recurring item' can be set up within Sage but that these must still be posted. See a later chapter for more details on recurring payments/receipts.

    Discrepancies between the bank statement and the company's own records of this nature should be dealt with by updating the company's records.

2   **Timing differences**

    This is a very common cause of discrepancies between the bank statement and the company's own records. Timing differences occur because the company will generally update its records before the bank has had the opportunity to process all transactions.

    Imagine the scenario where a company writes a cheque to a supplier on 1st March. The accounts clerk is likely to update the company's records (i.e. Sage) on that day. However, if the cheque was produced late in the afternoon it may not actually be posted until the following day and may not arrive at the supplier's address until two or three days after that. Weekends and public holidays can delay this further. It may then not be banked immediately by the supplier; it may take them two or three days to actually bank the cheque in their own branch. The cheque must then go through the banks' clearing system which may take 3–5 working days. Therefore the funds associated with that cheque (written on 1st March) may not actually be cleared out of the bank account until say 10th March or maybe later.

If a bank statement is sent to the company in this time it will not show the cheque payment, as it will not have been fully processed at the time the statement is produced. It will, however, have been recorded in the company's own accounts.

It is important therefore to undergo a process of bank reconciliation regularly to ensure that the only differences between the bank statement and the company's own records are caused by these timing differences (which can easily be accounted for), and not by the third reason for discrepancies, where an error has occurred.

3   **Errors**

It is perfectly possible for either the bank or (more likely) the company to have made an error in the course of producing their figures. We have already seen that the payment made to the Cricket League was incorrectly recorded as £55 instead of £85. You have already corrected this error, but had you not done so the reconciliation between the bank statement and Sage would have resulted in a discrepancy of £30.00. You would therefore have had to undertake further investigations into the cause of the error and then to correct it appropriately.

2   Performing a bank reconciliation using Sage

 Activity

Perform a bank reconciliation for TotalPhoto Ltd using the bank statement provided at the start of this chapter. Guidance follows.

From the **BANK** Module, click on the 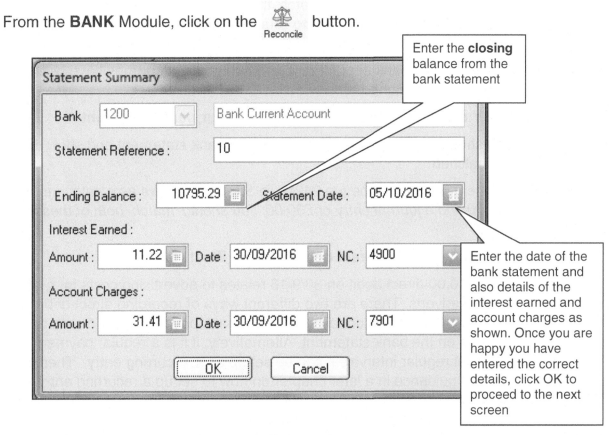 button.

Enter the **closing** balance from the bank statement

Enter the date of the bank statement and also details of the interest earned and account charges as shown. Once you are happy you have entered the correct details, click OK to proceed to the next screen

This screen also allows you to enter the summary of your Bank Statement. Notice here that you can enter the interest earned and any bank charges directly via this screen.

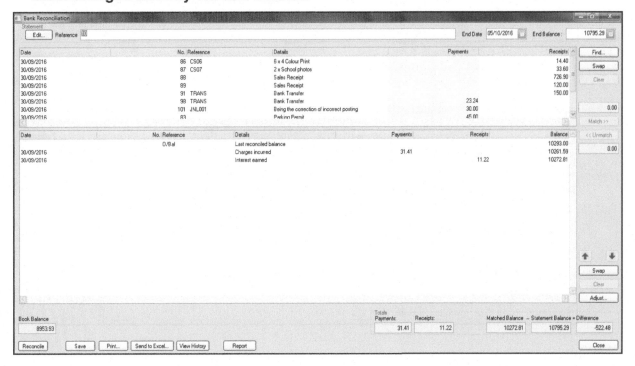

You now use this screen to 'match' the entries on your bank statement with the entries in Sage. **You do this by highlighting each entry in the Unmatched Items section and then pressing the** | Match >> | **button**.

Notice how the bank interest received and account charges have been automatically matched.

ONLY match the items that appear on your bank statement

You should find the following items on the bank statement and show them as 'matched'

Payment of £85.00 (cheque 242) – *in Sage this shows as a payment of £55.00 and a journal entry of £30.00; you should 'match' both of these items.*

How to record the direct debit to North West Radio

The £240.00 direct debit on 30/9/16 relates to advertising costs for a string of radio adverts. There are two different ways of recording direct debits on Sage. It can either be done as a manual bank payment each month once it appears on the bank statement. Alternatively, if it is a regular payment that is paid at regular intervals it can be set up as a 'recurring entry'. There is detailed guidance in a later chapter on how to set up a recurring entry. For the purposes of this bank reconciliation, you will need to record the direct debit as a 'bank payment' as follows.

Click on '**Adjust**' within the bank rec screen and then choose the option for bank payment and enter the details as shown below:

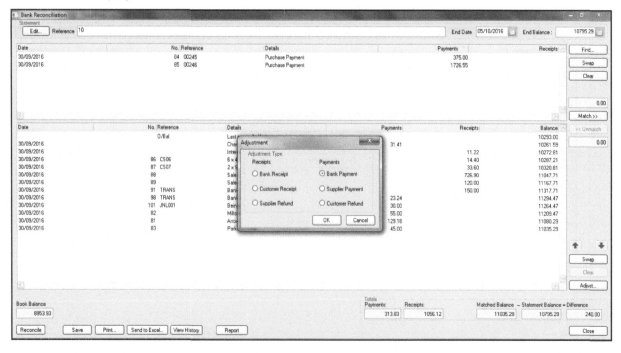

KAPLAN PUBLISHING

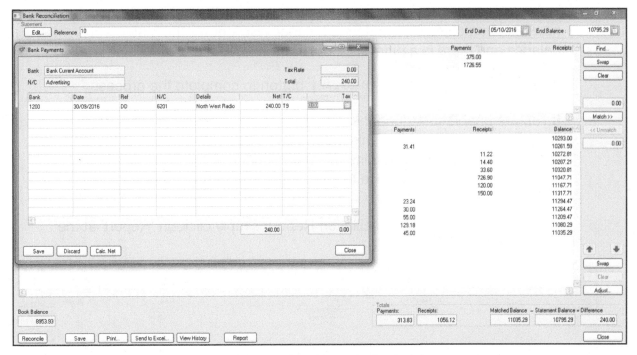

Click **Save** to process the direct debit through the bank current account. Notice that Sage will automatically match this item and it will now appear in the bottom window of the bank rec screen.

Once you have matched all the other items they will appear in the '**Matched Against Statement**' box as shown below:

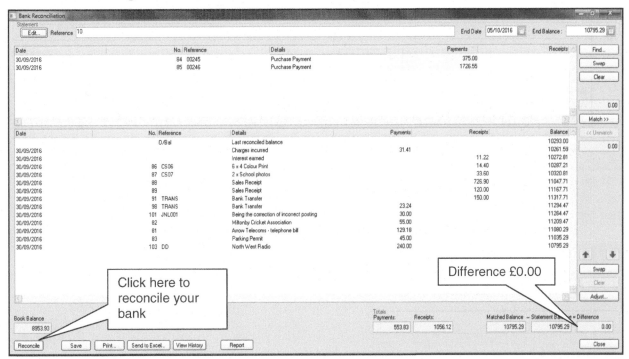

You can see here that the items which appear on the bank statement have now been matched. The matched balance now equals the statement balance and there is a difference of **NIL**.

You should now press the ⎡ Reconcile ⎤ button to complete the process.

If you are unable to reduce the difference to NIL, you can choose to click Save instead of reconcile. This means that Sage will retain all of the details entered so far regarding this particular bank rec. You can then make a note of the difference to investigate and return to the bank rec later.

To review your Bank Reconciliation Report, simply click on 'Report' at the bottom of the screen:

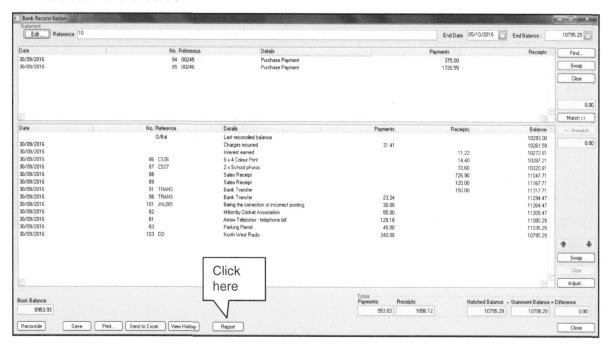

KAPLAN PUBLISHING

Your bank reconciliation report should now look like this:

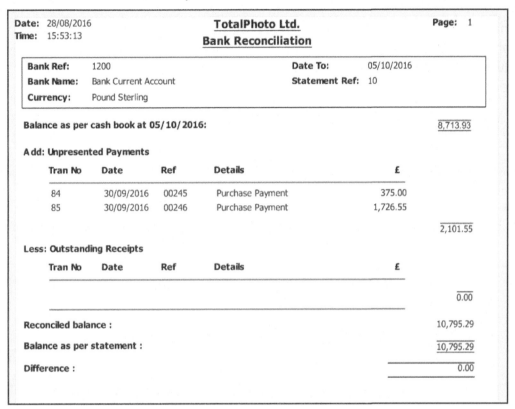

Date:	28/08/2016		**TotalPhoto Ltd.**				Page:	1
Time:	15:53:13		**Bank Reconciliation**					

Bank Ref:	1200			**Date To:**	05/10/2016
Bank Name:	Bank Current Account			**Statement Ref:**	10
Currency:	Pound Sterling				

Balance as per cash book at 05/10/2016: 8,713.93

Add: Unpresented Payments

Tran No	Date	Ref	Details	£
84	30/09/2016	00245	Purchase Payment	375.00
85	30/09/2016	00246	Purchase Payment	1,726.55
				2,101.55

Less: Outstanding Receipts

Tran No	Date	Ref	Details	£
				0.00

Reconciled balance :	10,795.29
Balance as per statement :	10,795.29
Difference :	0.00

The purpose of a bank reconciliation is to identify:

- Transactions which have been posted in the accounting system which have not appeared on the bank statement at the statement date.

- Transactions which appear on the bank statement which have not been accounted for in the accounting system.

The sum of these items will enable you to reconcile the actual bank balance with the balance on the bank account in the accounting system.

Following a bank reconciliation process in Sage, it is possible to run a report to list and total bank account postings which have not appeared on the bank statement. See Unreconciled Bank Transactions report.

The items on this report will continue to grow until a bank reconciliation is carried out again. When a new unreconciled bank statement is available and a new reconciliation is carried out, the available items for reconciliation/matching will be all transactions in the accounting system which have yet to be reconciled – as per the report.

Normally all of the transactions which appear on the bank statement, which have not been accounted for in the accounting system, will be created and posted/matched at the time of processing the reconciliation.

Very rarely there may be statement errors which need to be queried directly with the bank.

In our example, you may recall, there are two transactions within Sage which are yet to appear on the bank statement. These two items will be available for reconciliation when the next statement from the bank is received.

You can prove this yourself by running the unreconciled transactions report.

Date:	28/08/2016			**TotalPhoto Ltd.**				Page:	1
Time:	16:06:04			**Bank Report - Unreconciled**					

Date From : 01/10/2015
Date To : 30/09/2016

** NOTE: All values shown on this report are in the Bank Account's operating Currency **

Bank Code 1200   Bank Name : Bank Current Account

No	Type	Date	Ref	Details	Debit	Credit	Balance
84	PP	30/09/2016	00245	Purchase Payment		375.00	-375.00
85	PP	30/09/2016	00246	Purchase Payment		1,726.55	-1,726.55
				Bank Balance :		2,101.55	-2,101.55
						2,101.55	-2,101.55

Useful reports

ASSESSMENT CRITERIA	CONTENTS

<table>
<tr><td>

ASSESSMENT CRITERIA

Produce routine reports for customers and suppliers (5.1)

Produce routine reports from the general ledger (5.2)

</td><td>

CONTENTS

1 Introduction

2 Customer reports

3 Supplier reports

4 Bank reports

5 Journal Day Book and Audit Trail reports

</td></tr>
</table>

1 Introduction

Although it is possible to create and produce your own Sage reports, there are a number of extremely useful report layouts already set up within Sage.

You have already seen a number of these throughout the manual.

You should now make yourself familiar with these, plus the other reports shown below. **These reports are for demonstration purposes only and the figures contained in them are not specifically relevant to the case study you have been working on.**

Note that there are many other reports within Sage; you should take the time to examine all of these to find the reports that will best suit your business.

Have a go at practising generating reports using the **REPORTS** icon within each module. Ensure you are comfortable with exporting the report from Sage to create a **PDF** version. This can easily be done by clicking on **EXPORT** (rather than print) each time you generate a new report. Remember to save the file as a PDF type. This may be required as part of your actual computer based assessment process so it's an essential part of your studies.

You can practise as much as you like in order to familiarise yourself with the process.

2 Customer reports

Aged Debtors Analysis

Date:	01/09/2016		**TotalPhoto Ltd.**			Page:	1
Time:	00:14:44		**Aged Debtors Analysis (Detailed)**				

Date From:	01/01/1980			Customer From:	
Date To:	30/09/2016			Customer To:	ZZZZZZZZ

Include future transactions: No
Exclude later payments: No

** NOTE: All report values are shown in Base Currency, unless otherwise indicated **

| A/C: | CAM004 | Name: | Campbell & Dunn | | Contact: | | | | Tel: | |

No	Type	Date	Ref	Details	Balance	Future	Current	Period 1	Period 2	Period 3	Older
10	SI	01/10/2015	O/Bal	Opening Balance	2,056.85	0.00	0.00	0.00	0.00	0.00	2,056.85
72	SI	30/09/2016	6	Corporate	54.00	0.00	54.00	0.00	0.00	0.00	0.00
				Totals:	2,110.85	0.00	54.00	0.00	0.00	0.00	2,056.85

Turnover: 2,101.85
Credit Limit £ 2,500.00

| A/C: | HAS004 | Name: | Mr W Haslam | | Contact: | | | | Tel: | |

No	Type	Date	Ref	Details	Balance	Future	Current	Period 1	Period 2	Period 3	Older
7	SI	01/10/2015	O/Bal	Opening Balance	309.85	0.00	0.00	0.00	0.00	0.00	309.85
68	SI	30/09/2016	2	Individuals & Families	29.40	0.00	29.40	0.00	0.00	0.00	0.00
73	SI	30/09/2016	7	Individuals & Families	14.40	0.00	14.40	0.00	0.00	0.00	0.00
				Totals:	353.65	0.00	43.80	0.00	0.00	0.00	309.85

Turnover: 346.35
Credit Limit £ 500.00

| A/C: | LUL002 | Name: | Lullabies Nursery | | Contact: | | | | Tel: | |

No	Type	Date	Ref	Details	Balance	Future	Current	Period 1	Period 2	Period 3	Older
71	SI	30/09/2016	5	Nurseries & Schools	120.00	0.00	120.00	0.00	0.00	0.00	0.00
111	SP	30/09/2016	CANCEL	Cancelled Cheque	726.90	0.00	726.90	0.00	0.00	0.00	0.00
				Totals:	846.90	0.00	846.90	0.00	0.00	0.00	0.00

Turnover: 826.90
Credit Limit £ 1,500.00

| A/C: | PAR006 | Name: | Miss S Pargenter | | Contact: | | | | Tel: | |

No	Type	Date	Ref	Details	Balance	Future	Current	Period 1	Period 2	Period 3	Older
12	SI	01/10/2015	O/Bal	Opening Balance	650.00	0.00	0.00	0.00	0.00	0.00	650.00
69	SI	30/09/2016	3	Individuals & Families	14.40	0.00	14.40	0.00	0.00	0.00	0.00
74	SC	30/09/2016		Faulty	-14.40	0.00	-14.40	0.00	0.00	0.00	0.00
				Totals:	650.00	0.00	0.00	0.00	0.00	0.00	650.00

Turnover: 650.00
Credit Limit £ 1,000.00

| A/C: | POP002 | Name: | Mrs H Poppy | | Contact: | | | | Tel: | |

No	Type	Date	Ref	Details	Balance	Future	Current	Period 1	Period 2	Period 3	Older
67	SI	30/09/2016	1	Individuals & Families	126.00	0.00	126.00	0.00	0.00	0.00	0.00
				Totals:	126.00	0.00	126.00	0.00	0.00	0.00	0.00

Turnover: 325.00
Credit Limit £ 500.00

| A/C: | SMI009 | Name: | Mr A Smith | | Contact: | | | | Tel: | |

No	Type	Date	Ref	Details	Balance	Future	Current	Period 1	Period 2	Period 3	Older
70	SI	30/09/2016	4	Weddings	720.00	0.00	720.00	0.00	0.00	0.00	0.00
				Totals:	720.00	0.00	720.00	0.00	0.00	0.00	0.00

Turnover: 600.00
Credit Limit £ 1,000.00

| | | | | Grand Totals: | 4,807.40 | 0.00 | 1,790.70 | 0.00 | 0.00 | 0.00 | 3,016.70 |

Shows a list of debtors with analysis of how long the debts have been in existence

Day Books – Customer Invoices

Date:	28/08/2016					TotalPhoto Ltd.				Page:	1
Time:	16:14:02					Day Books: Customer Invoices (Detailed)					

Date From:	01/01/1980			Customer From:	
Date To:	31/12/2019			Customer To:	ZZZZZZZZ
Transaction From:	1			N/C From:	
Transaction To:	99,999,999			N/C To:	99999999
Dept From:	0				
Dept To:	999				

Tran No.	Type	Date	A/C Ref	N/C	Inv Ref	Dept.	Details	Net Amount	Tax Amount	T/C	Gross Amount	V	B
7	SI	01/10/2015	HAS004	9998	O/Bal	0	Opening Balance	309.85	0.00	T9	309.85	-	-
8	SI	01/10/2015	POP002	9998	O/Bal	0	Opening Balance	220.00	0.00	T9	220.00	-	-
9	SI	01/10/2015	PAS002	9998	O/Bal	0	Opening Balance	89.50	0.00	T9	89.50	-	-
10	SI	01/10/2015	CAM004	9998	O/Bal	0	Opening Balance	2,056.85	0.00	T9	2,056.85	-	-
11	SI	01/10/2015	LUL002	9998	O/Bal	0	Opening Balance	726.90	0.00	T9	726.90	-	-
12	SI	01/10/2015	PAR006	9998	O/Bal	0	Opening Balance	650.00	0.00	T9	650.00	-	-
67	SI	30/09/2016	POP002	4000	1	0	Individuals & Families	105.00	21.00	T1	126.00	N	-
68	SI	30/09/2016	HAS004	4000	2	0	Individuals & Families	24.50	4.90	T1	29.40	N	-
69	SI	30/09/2016	PAR006	4000	3	0	Individuals & Families	12.00	2.40	T1	14.40	N	-
70	SI	30/09/2016	SMI009	4001	4	0	Weddings	600.00	120.00	T1	720.00	N	-
71	SI	30/09/2016	LUL002	4003	5	0	Nurseries & Schools	100.00	20.00	T1	120.00	N	-
72	SI	30/09/2016	CAM004	4002	6	0	Corporate	45.00	9.00	T1	54.00	N	-
73	SI	30/09/2016	HAS004	4000	7	0	Individuals & Families	12.00	2.40	T1	14.40	N	-
							Totals:	4,951.60	179.70		5,131.30		

Shows a list of all invoices produced including the Net, VAT and Gross Amounts

Customer Activity – Detailed

Date:	01/09/2016		**TotalPhoto Ltd.**		Page:	1
Time:	00:10:54		**Customer Activity (Detailed)**			

Date From:	01/01/1980		Customer From:	
Date To:	30/09/2016		Customer To:	ZZZZZZZZ
Transaction From:	1		N/C From:	
Transaction To:	110		N/C To:	99999999
Inc b/fwd transaction:	No		Dept From:	0
Exc later payment:	No		Dept To:	999

** NOTE: All report values are shown in Base Currency, unless otherwise indicated **

A/C: CAM004   Name: Campbell & Dunn   Contact: Tel:

No	Type	Date	Ref	N/C	Details	Dept	T/C	Value	O/S	Debit	Credit	V	B
10	SI	01/10/2015	O/Bal	9998	Opening Balance	0	T9	2,056.85 *	2,056.85	2,056.85		-	-
72	SI	30/09/2016	6	4002	Corporate	0	T1	54.00 *	54.00	54.00		N	-
					Totals:			2,110.85	2,110.85	2,110.85			

Amount Outstanding	2,110.85
Amount Paid this period	0.00
Credit Limit £	2,500.00
Turnover YTD	2,101.85

A/C: HAS004   Name: Mr W Haslam   Contact: Tel:

No	Type	Date	Ref	N/C	Details	Dept	T/C	Value	O/S	Debit	Credit	V	B
7	SI	01/10/2015	O/Bal	9998	Opening Balance	0	T9	309.85 *	309.85	309.85		-	-
68	SI	30/09/2016	2	4000	Individuals & Families	0	T1	29.40 *	29.40	29.40		N	-
73	SI	30/09/2016	7	4000	Individuals & Families	0	T1	14.40 *	14.40	14.40		N	-
					Totals:			353.65	353.65	353.65			

Amount Outstanding	353.65
Amount Paid this period	0.00
Credit Limit £	500.00
Turnover YTD	346.35

A/C: LUL002   Name: Lullabies Nursery   Contact: Tel:

No	Type	Date	Ref	N/C	Details	Dept	T/C	Value	O/S	Debit	Credit	V	B
11	SI	01/10/2015	O/Bal	9998	Opening Balance	0	T9	726.90		726.90		-	-
71	SI	30/09/2016	5	4003	Nurseries & Schools	0	T1	120.00 *	120.00	120.00		N	-
88	SR	30/09/2016	CANCEL	1200	Sales Receipt	0	T9	726.90			726.90	-	R
					Totals:			120.00	120.00	846.90	726.90		

Amount Outstanding	120.00
Amount Paid this period	0.00
Credit Limit £	1,500.00
Turnover YTD	826.90

A/C: PAR006   Name: Miss S Pargenter   Contact: Tel:

No	Type	Date	Ref	N/C	Details	Dept	T/C	Value	O/S	Debit	Credit	V	B
12	SI	01/10/2015	O/Bal	9998	Opening Balance	0	T9	650.00 *	650.00	650.00		-	-
69	SI	30/09/2016	3	4000	Individuals & Families	0	T1	14.40 *	14.40	14.40		N	-
74	SC	30/09/2016		4000	Faulty	0	T1	14.40 *	-14.40		14.40	N	-
					Totals:			650.00	650.00	664.40	14.40		

Amount Outstanding	650.00
Amount Paid this period	0.00
Credit Limit £	1,000.00
Turnover YTD	650.00

| Date: | 01/09/2016 | **TotalPhoto Ltd.** | Page: | 2 |
| Time: | 00:10:54 | **Customer Activity (Detailed)** | | |

| A/C: | PAS002 | Name: | Mrs T Pashby | | Contact: | | | | Tel: | | | |

No	Type	Date	Ref	N/C	Details	Dept	T/C	Value	O/S	Debit	Credit	V	B
9	SI	01/10/2015	O/Bal	9998	Opening Balance	0	T9	89.50		89.50		.	.
102	SC	30/09/2016	BADDBT	8100	Bad Debt Write Off	0	T9	89.50			89.50	.	.
					Totals:			0.00	0.00	89.50	89.50		

Amount Outstanding	0.00
Amount Paid this period	0.00
Credit Limit £	500.00
Turnover YTD	179.00

| A/C: | POP002 | Name: | Mrs H Poppy | | Contact: | | | | Tel: | | | |

No	Type	Date	Ref	N/C	Details	Dept	T/C	Value	O/S	Debit	Credit	V	B
8	SI	01/10/2015	O/Bal	9998	Opening Balance	0	T9	220.00		220.00		.	.
67	SI	30/09/2016	1	4000	Individuals & Families	0	T1	126.00 *	126.00	126.00		N	.
89	SR	30/09/2016		1200	Sales Receipt	0	T9	120.00			120.00	.	R
106	SR	30/09/2016		1200	Sales Receipt	0	T9	100.00			100.00	.	N
					Totals:			126.00	126.00	346.00	220.00		

Amount Outstanding	126.00
Amount Paid this period	220.00
Credit Limit £	500.00
Turnover YTD	325.00

| A/C: | SMI009 | Name: | Mr A Smith | | Contact: | | | | Tel: | | | |

No	Type	Date	Ref	N/C	Details	Dept	T/C	Value	O/S	Debit	Credit	V	B
70	SI	30/09/2016	4	4001	Weddings	0	T1	720.00 *	720.00	720.00		N	.
					Totals:			720.00	720.00	720.00			

Amount Outstanding	720.00
Amount Paid this period	0.00
Credit Limit £	1,000.00
Turnover YTD	600.00

Shows all transactions for customers (e.g. purchases and receipts)

Customer Address List

| Date: | 28/08/2016 | **TotalPhoto Ltd.** | Page: | 1 |
| Time: | 16:19:33 | **Customer Address List** | | |

Customer From:
Customer To: ZZZZZZZZ

A/C	Name & Address	Contact Name	Telephone	Fax
CAM004	Campbell & Dunn 12 The Beaches Miltonby Lancashire LN87 9PP			
HAS004	Mr W Haslam 22 Brown Street Miltonby Lancashire LN87 6FD			
LUL002	Lullabies Nursery 104 Victoria Road Miltonby Lancashire LN87 5PS			
PAR006	Miss S Pargenter 11 Alexandra Park Miltonby Lancashire LN87 2WD			

Shows address details, contact name etc for customers

3 Supplier reports

Aged Creditors Analysis

Date: 01/09/2016 **Time:** 00:15:27

TotalPhoto Ltd.
Aged Creditors Analysis (Detailed)

Page: 1

Date From:	01/01/1980
Date To:	30/09/2016

Supplier From:	
Supplier To:	ZZZZZZZZ

Include future transactions: No
Exclude later payments: No

** NOTE: All report values are shown in Base Currency, unless otherwise indicated **

A/C: AP004   **Name:** Arthur's Photographic Equipment Ltd.   **Contact:** Jennie Reeves   **Tel:** 0121 299 0192

No:	Type	Date	Ref	Details	Balance	Future	Current	Period 1	Period 2	Period 3	Older
6	PI	30/09/2016	O/Bal	Opening Balance	11,275.00	0.00	11,275.00	0.00	0.00	0.00	0.00
80	PC	30/09/2016	134C	Faulty return of	-2,531.99	0.00	-2,531.99	0.00	0.00	0.00	0.00
				Totals:	8,743.01	0.00	8,743.01	0.00	0.00	0.00	0.00

Turnover: 9,165.01
Credit Limit £ 20,000.00

A/C: MF001   **Name:** Mackay Films Ltd   **Contact:** Carl Richardson   **Tel:** 01828 827 493

No:	Type	Date	Ref	Details	Balance	Future	Current	Period 1	Period 2	Period 3	Older
1	PI	30/09/2016	O/Bal	Opening Balance	345.36	0.00	345.36	0.00	0.00	0.00	0.00
75	PI	30/09/2016	1341	Film	250.51	0.00	250.51	0.00	0.00	0.00	0.00
				Totals:	595.87	0.00	595.87	0.00	0.00	0.00	0.00

Turnover: 554.12
Credit Limit £ 2,500.00

A/C: MP002   **Name:** Mills Paper Products   **Contact:** Mr Shaun Squire   **Tel:** 01726 378 918

No:	Type	Date	Ref	Details	Balance	Future	Current	Period 1	Period 2	Period 3	Older
4	PI	30/09/2016	O/Bal	Opening Balance	4,920.30	0.00	4,920.30	0.00	0.00	0.00	0.00
79	PI	30/09/2016	10092	Paper	195.02	0.00	195.02	0.00	0.00	0.00	0.00
				Totals:	5,115.32	0.00	5,115.32	0.00	0.00	0.00	0.00

Turnover: 5,082.82
Credit Limit £ 8,000.00

A/C: OI001   **Name:** Octopus Inks Ltd   **Contact:** Sheila Cribbley   **Tel:** 0191 252 4132

No:	Type	Date	Ref	Details	Balance	Future	Current	Period 1	Period 2	Period 3	Older
5	PI	30/09/2016	O/Bal	Opening Balance	550.20	0.00	550.20	0.00	0.00	0.00	0.00
78	PI	30/09/2016	2203	Cartridges & Toners	371.14	0.00	371.14	0.00	0.00	0.00	0.00
				Totals:	921.34	0.00	921.34	0.00	0.00	0.00	0.00

Turnover: 859.48
Credit Limit £ 2,500.00

A/C: SC003   **Name:** The Stationery Cupboard   **Contact:** Alan Pensill   **Tel:** 01482 417378

No:	Type	Date	Ref	Details	Balance	Future	Current	Period 1	Period 2	Period 3	Older
76	PI	30/09/2016	209	Stationery	17.58	0.00	17.58	0.00	0.00	0.00	0.00
77	PI	30/09/2016	216	Stationery	94.70	0.00	94.70	0.00	0.00	0.00	0.00
				Totals:	112.28	0.00	112.28	0.00	0.00	0.00	0.00

Turnover: 468.57
Credit Limit £ 1,000.00

				Grand Totals:	15,487.82	0.00	15,487.82	0.00	0.00	0.00	0.00

Shows the outstanding creditor balances and the how long the debts have been in existence

Supplier Activity Report

Date:	01/09/2016	**TotalPhoto Ltd.**	**Page:** 1
Time:	00:15:55	**Supplier Activity (Detailed)**	

Date From:	01/01/1980	**Supplier From:**	
Date To:	30/09/2016	**Supplier To:**	ZZZZZZZZ
Transaction From:	1	**N/C From:**	
Transaction To:	99,999,999	**N/C To:**	99999999
Inc b/fwd transaction:	No	**Dept From:**	0
Exc later payment:	No	**Dept To:**	999

** NOTE: All report values are shown in Base Currency, unless otherwise indicated **

A/C: AP004 **Name:** Arthur's Photographic Equipment Ltd. **Contact:** Jennie Reeves **Tel:** 0121 299 0192

No	Type	Date	Ref	N/C	Details	Dept	T/C	Value	O/S	Debit	Credit	V	B
6	PI	30/09/2016	O/Bal	9998	Opening Balance	0	T9	11,275.00 *	11,275.00		11,275.00	-	-
80	PC	30/09/2016	134C	0032	Faulty return of Camera	0	T1	2,531.99 *	-2,531.99	2,531.99		N	-
					Totals:			8,743.01	8,743.01	2,531.99	11,275.00		

Amount Outstanding	8,743.01
Amount paid this period	0.00
Credit Limit £	20,000.00
Turnover YTD	9,165.01

A/C: KF001 **Name:** K2 Films Ltd. **Contact:** Kim Nakajima **Tel:** 0207 867 6599

No	Type	Date	Ref	N/C	Details	Dept	T/C	Value	O/S	Debit	Credit	V	B
2	PI	30/09/2016	O/Bal	9998	Opening Balance	0	T9	1,726.55	0.00		1,726.55	-	-
85	PP	30/09/2016	00246	1200	Purchase Payment	0	T9	1,726.55	0.00	1,726.55		-	N
					Totals:			0.00	0.00	1,726.55	1,726.55		

Amount Outstanding	0.00
Amount paid this period	1,726.55
Credit Limit £	5,000.00
Turnover YTD	1,726.55

A/C: MF001 **Name:** Mackay Films Ltd **Contact:** Carl Richardson **Tel:** 01828 827 493

No	Type	Date	Ref	N/C	Details	Dept	T/C	Value	O/S	Debit	Credit	V	B
1	PI	30/09/2016	O/Bal	9998	Opening Balance	0	T9	345.36 *	345.36		345.36	-	-
75	PI	30/09/2016	1341	5000	Film	0	T1	250.51 *	250.51		250.51	N	-
					Totals:			595.87	595.87	0.00	595.87		

Amount Outstanding	595.87
Amount paid this period	0.00
Credit Limit £	2,500.00
Turnover YTD	554.12

A/C: MP002 **Name:** Mills Paper Products **Contact:** Mr Shaun Squire **Tel:** 01726 378 918

No	Type	Date	Ref	N/C	Details	Dept	T/C	Value	O/S	Debit	Credit	V	B
4	PI	30/09/2016	O/Bal	9998	Opening Balance	0	T9	4,920.30 *	4,920.30		4,920.30	-	-
79	PI	30/09/2016	10092	5001	Paper	0	T1	195.02 *	195.02		195.02	N	-
					Totals:			5,115.32	5,115.32	0.00	5,115.32		

Amount Outstanding	5,115.32
Amount paid this period	0.00
Credit Limit £	8,000.00
Turnover YTD	5,082.82

A/C: OI001 **Name:** Octopus Inks Ltd **Contact:** Sheila Cribbley **Tel:** 0191 252 4132

No	Type	Date	Ref	N/C	Details	Dept	T/C	Value	O/S	Debit	Credit	V	B
5	PI	30/09/2016	O/Bal	9998	Opening Balance	0	T9	550.20 *	550.20		550.20	-	-
78	PI	30/09/2016	2203	5002	Cartridges & Toners	0	T1	371.14 *	371.14		371.14	N	-
					Totals:			921.34	921.34	0.00	921.34		

Amount Outstanding	921.34
Amount paid this period	0.00
Credit Limit £	2,500.00
Turnover YTD	859.48

Date:	01/09/2016				**TotalPhoto Ltd.**				Page:	2			
Time:	00:15:55				**Supplier Activity (Detailed)**								

A/C:	SC003	Name:	The Stationery Cupboard			Contact:	Alan Pensill			Tel:	01482 417378		

No	Type	Date	Ref	N/C	Details	Dept	T/C	Value	O/S	Debit	Credit	V	B
3	PI	30/09/2016	O/Bal	9998	Opening Balance	0	T9	375.00	0.00		375.00	-	-
76	PI	30/09/2016	209	5003	Stationery	0	T1	17.58 *	17.58		17.58	N	-
77	PI	30/09/2016	216	5003	Stationery	0	T1	94.70 *	94.70		94.70	N	-
84	PP	30/09/2016	00245	1200	Purchase Payment	0	T9	375.00	0.00	375.00		-	N
						Totals:		112.28	112.28	375.00	487.28		

Amount Outstanding	112.28
Amount paid this period	375.00
Credit Limit £	1,000.00
Turnover YTD	468.57

Shows all transactions for a single, or range of, suppliers, including purchases, returns, payments etc

Day Book Supplier Invoices

Date:	28/08/2016				**TotalPhoto Ltd.**				Page:	1
Time:	16:26:19				**Day Books: Supplier Invoices (Detailed)**					

Date From:	01/01/1980	Supplier From:	
Date To:	31/12/2019	Supplier To:	ZZZZZZZ

Transaction From:	1	N/C From:	
Transaction To:	99,999,999	N/C To:	99999999

Dept From:	0
Dept To:	999

Tran No.	Type	Date	A/C Ref	N/C	Inv Ref	Dept	Details	Net Amount	Tax Amount	T/C	Gross Amount	V	B
1	PI	30/09/2016	MF001	9998	O/Bal	0	Opening Balance	345.36	0.00	T9	345.36	-	-
2	PI	30/09/2016	KF001	9998	O/Bal	0	Opening Balance	1,726.55	0.00	T9	1,726.55	-	-
3	PI	30/09/2016	SC003	9998	O/Bal	0	Opening Balance	375.00	0.00	T9	375.00	-	-
4	PI	30/09/2016	MP002	9998	O/Bal	0	Opening Balance	4,920.30	0.00	T9	4,920.30	-	-
5	PI	30/09/2016	OI001	9998	O/Bal	0	Opening Balance	550.20	0.00	T9	550.20	-	-
6	PI	30/09/2016	AP004	9998	O/Bal	0	Opening Balance	11,275.00	0.00	T9	11,275.00	-	-
75	PI	30/09/2016	MF001	5000	1341	0	Film	208.76	41.75	T1	250.51	N	-
76	PI	30/09/2016	SC003	5003	209	0	Stationery	14.65	2.93	T1	17.58	N	-
77	PI	30/09/2016	SC003	5003	216	0	Stationery	78.92	15.78	T1	94.70	N	-
78	PI	30/09/2016	OI001	5002	2203	0	Cartridges & Toners	309.28	61.86	T1	371.14	N	-
79	PI	30/09/2016	MP002	5001	10092	0	Paper	162.52	32.50	T1	195.02	N	-
							Totals	19,966.54	154.82		20,121.36		

Shows the list of all invoices received.

Supplier Details List

Date: 28/08/2016		**TotalPhoto Ltd.**		**Page:** 1
Time: 16:27:35		**Supplier Address List**		

Supplier From:
Supplier To: ZZZZZZZZ

A/C	Name	Contact	Telephone	Fax
AP004	Arthur's Photographic Equipment Ltd. 77 Overton Lane Birmingham BM97 8YK	Jennie Reeves	0121 299 0192	
KF001	K2 Films Ltd. Tokyo House 72 - 84 Great Milne Street Lodon WC4 6DD	Kim Nakajima	0207 867 6599	
MF001	Mackay Films Ltd 33 West Parade Miltonby Lancashire LN87 7HD	Carl Richardson	01828 827 493	
MP002	Mills Paper Products 405 Ream Road Bradford West Yorkshire BD5 6QA	Mr Shaun Squire	01726 378 918	

Shows a list of suppliers with contact details

4 Bank reports

Day Books: Bank Payments

Date: 28/08/2016		**TotalPhoto Ltd.**		**Page:** 1
Time: 16:37:24		**Day Books: Bank Payments (Detailed)**		

Date From: 01/01/1980		Bank From: 1200	
Date To: 31/12/2019		Bank To: 1200	
Transaction From: 1		N/C From:	
Transaction To: 99,999,999		N/C To: 99999999	
Dept From: 0			
Dept To: 999			

Bank: 1200   **Currency:** Pound Sterling

No	Type	N/C	Date	Ref	Details	Dept	Net £	Tax £ T/C	Gross £ V B	Bank Rec. Date
81	BP	7502	30/09/2016		Arrow Telecoms -	0	107.65	21.53 T1	129.18 N R	05/10/2016
82	BP	6201	30/09/2016		Miltonby Cricket	0	55.00	0.00 T9	55.00 - R	05/10/2016
83	BP	7304	30/09/2016		Parking Permit	0	45.00	0.00 T0	45.00 N R	05/10/2016
103	BP	6201	30/09/2016	DD	North West Radio	0	240.00	0.00 T9	240.00 - R	05/10/2016
105	BP	7901	30/09/2016		Charges incurred	0	31.41	0.00 T2	31.41 N R	05/10/2016
						Totals £	479.06	21.53	500.59	

Shows all payments from the chosen bank account

Day Books: Bank Receipts

															Bank Rec.

Date: 28/08/2016
Time: 16:38:53

TotalPhoto Ltd.
Day Books: Bank Receipts (Detailed)

Page: 1

Date From: 01/01/1980
Date To: 31/12/2019

Bank From: 1200
Bank To: 1200

Transaction From: 1
Transaction To: 99,999,999

N/C From:
N/C To: 99999999

Dept From: 0
Dept To: 999

Bank: 1200   Currency: Pound Sterling

No	Type	N/C	Date	Ref	Details	Dept	Net £	Tax £ T/C	Gross £ V B	Bank Rec. Date
86	BR	4000	30/09/2016	CS06	6 x 4 Colour Print	0	12.00	2.40 T1	14.40 N R	05/10/2016
87	BR	4003	30/09/2016	CS07	2 x School photos	0	28.00	5.60 T1	33.60 N R	05/10/2016
104	BR	4900	30/09/2016		Interest earned	0	11.22	0.00 T2	11.22 N R	05/10/2016
						Totals £	51.22	8.00	59.22	

Shows all receipts to the chosen bank account

Similar reports are available for cash, and credit card, payments and receipts

Reconciled Transactions

Date: 28/08/2016
Time: 16:40:33

TotalPhoto Ltd.
Bank Reconciled Transactions

Page: 1

Bank Reconciled On 28/08/2016

No	Type	Date	A/C	N/C	Dept	Ref	Details	Net	Tax	T/C
29	JD	01/10/2015	1200	1200	0	O/Bal	Opening Balance	10,293.00	0.00	T9

Bank Reconciled On 05/10/2016

No	Type	Date	A/C	N/C	Dept	Ref	Details	Net	Tax	T/C
81	BP	30/09/2016	1200	7502	0		Arrow Telecoms -	107.65	21.53	T1
82	BP	30/09/2016	1200	6201	0		Miltonby Cricket	55.00	0.00	T9
83	BP	30/09/2016	1200	7304	0		Parking Permit	45.00	0.00	T0
86	BR	30/09/2016	1200	4000	0	CS06	6 x 4 Colour Print	12.00	2.40	T1
87	BR	30/09/2016	1200	4003	0	CS07	2 x School photos	28.00	5.60	T1
88	SR	30/09/2016	LUL002	1200	0		Sales Receipt	726.90	0.00	T9
89	SR	30/09/2016	POP002	1200	0		Sales Receipt	120.00	0.00	T9
91	JD	30/09/2016	1200	1200	0	TRANS	Bank Transfer	150.00	0.00	T9
98	JC	30/09/2016	1200	1200	0	TRANS	Bank Transfer	23.24	0.00	T9
101	JC	30/09/2016	1200	1200	0	JNL001	Being the correction of	30.00	0.00	T9
103	BP	30/09/2016	1200	6201	0	DD	North West Radio	240.00	0.00	T9
104	BR	30/09/2016	1200	4900	0		Interest earned	11.22	0.00	T2
105	BP	30/09/2016	1200	7901	0		Charges incurred	31.41	0.00	T2

Shows all bank transactions that have been successfully matched and reconciled to the bank statement

Day Book: Supplier Payments

Date:	28/08/2016			TotalPhoto Ltd.				Page:	1
Time:	16:41:50			Day Books: Supplier Payments (Detailed)					

Date From:	01/01/1980		Bank From:	1200
Date To:	31/12/2019		Bank To:	1200

Transaction From:	1		Supplier From:	
Transaction To:	99,999,999		Supplier To:	ZZZZZZZZ

Bank   1200   Currency   Pound Sterling

No	Type	A/C	Date	Ref	Details	Net £	Tax	£ T/C	Gross £ V B	Bank Rec. Date
84	PP	SC003	30/09/2016	00245	Purchase Payment	375.00	0.00	T9	375.00 -	N
			30/09/2016	O/Bal	375.00 to PI 3					
85	PP	KF001	30/09/2016	00246	Purchase Payment	1,726.55	0.00	T9	1,726.55 -	N
			30/09/2016	O/Bal	1726.55 to PI 2					
					Totals £	2,101.55	0.00		2,101.55	

Shows all payments made to suppliers

Day Book: Customer Receipts

Date:	28/08/2016			TotalPhoto Ltd.				Page:	1
Time:	16:43:24			Day Books: Customer Receipts (Detailed)					

Date From:	01/01/1980		Bank From:	1200
Date To:	31/12/2019		Bank To:	1200

Transaction From:	1		Customer From:	
Transaction To:	99,999,999		Customer To:	ZZZZZZZZ

Bank   1200   Currency   Pound Sterling

No	Type	A/C	Date	Ref	Details	Net £	Tax	£ T/C	Gross £ V B	Bank Rec. Date
88	SR	LUL002	30/09/2016		Sales Receipt	726.90	0.00	T9	726.90 -	R 05/10/2016
			30/09/2016	O/Bal	726.90 to SI 11					
89	SR	POP002	30/09/2016		Sales Receipt	120.00	0.00	T9	120.00 -	R 05/10/2016
			30/09/2016	O/Bal	120.00 to SI 8					
					Totals £	846.90	0.00		846.90	

Shows all receipts from customers

Unreconciled Payments Report

Date:	28/08/2016		TotalPhoto Ltd.		Page:	1
Time:	16:44:37		Unreconciled Payments			

Date From:	01/01/1980		Bank From:	1200
Date To:	31/12/2019		Bank To:	1200

Transaction From:	1	
Transaction To:	99,999,999	

Bank   1200   Bank Account Name   Bank Current Account   Currency   Pound Sterling

No	Type	Date	Ref	Details	Amount £
84	PP	30/09/2016	00245	Purchase Payment	375.00
85	PP	30/09/2016	00246	Purchase Payment	1,726.55
				Total £	2,101.55

Shows all payments which have not been matched and reconciled against a bank statement

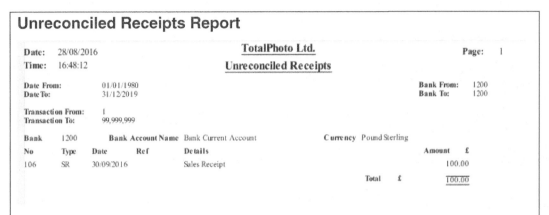

Unreconciled Receipts Report

Shows all receipts which have not been matched and reconciled against a bank statement

---

5 Journal Day Book and Audit Trail reports

As you are familiarising yourself with the various reports within each of the modules, you will see that the majority of them are quite logical in terms of where to find them. For example, the Sales Day Book is in Customers, Reports, Day Book reports.

One report that you may be required to print off in your UACS assessment but that doesn't necessarily sound familiar is the 'Journal Day Book'. This report details all transactions that have been entered onto Sage via a journal. The following shows where to find it:

Click on the 'Company' module and then 'Reports' at the top of the screen:

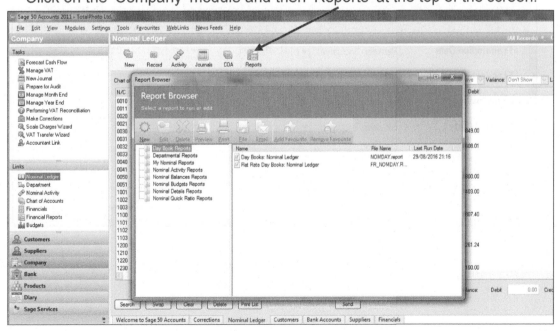

From this screen, select 'Day Book Reports' followed by 'Day Books: Nominal Ledger'

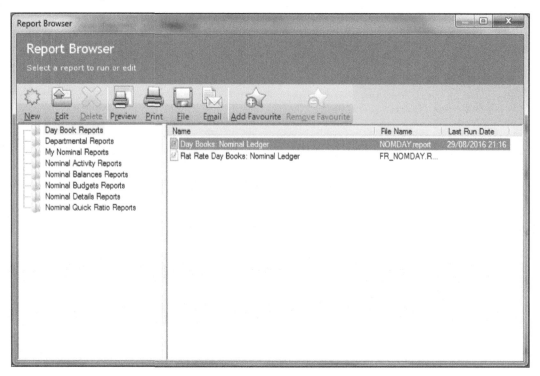

This screen will appear; you can amend the dates for a specific range dependent on what you want the report to show. (You can also do this for transaction numbers and nominal codes too.)

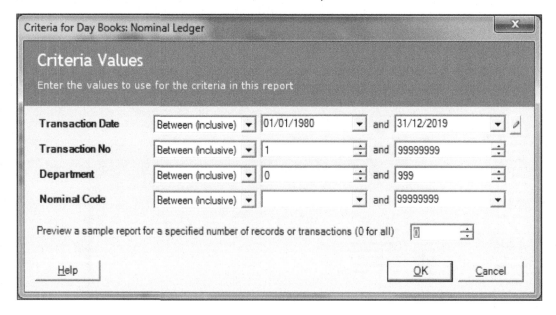

This is how the 'Journal Day Book' will look:

Date: 01/09/2016   **TotalPhoto Ltd.**   **Page:** 1

Time: 00:28:01   **Day Books: Nominal Ledger**

Date From: 01/01/1980   **N/C From:**
Date To: 31/12/2019   **N/C To:** 99999999

Transaction From: 1   **Dept From:** 0
Transaction To: 110   **Dept To:** 999

No	Type	N/C	Date	Ref	Ex.Ref	Details	Dept	T/C	Debit	Credit	V	B
13	JD	0050	01/10/2015	O/Bal		Opening Balance	0	T9	21,800.00		-	-
14	JC	9998	01/10/2015	O/Bal		Opening Balance	0	T9		21,800.00	-	-
15	JC	0051	01/10/2015	O/Bal		Opening Balance	0	T9		5,450.00	-	-
16	JD	9998	01/10/2015	O/Bal		Opening Balance	0	T9	5,450.00		-	-
17	JD	0030	01/10/2015	O/Bal		Opening Balance	0	T9	4,849.00		-	-
18	JC	9998	01/10/2015	O/Bal		Opening Balance	0	T9		4,849.00	-	-
19	JC	0031	01/10/2015	O/Bal		Opening Balance	0	T9		921.00	-	-
20	JD	9998	01/10/2015	O/Bal		Opening Balance	0	T9	921.00		-	-
21	JD	0032	01/10/2015	O/Bal		Opening Balance	0	T9	22,718.00		-	-
22	JC	9998	01/10/2015	O/Bal		Opening Balance	0	T9		22,718.00	-	-
23	JC	0033	01/10/2015	O/Bal		Opening Balance	0	T9		4,316.00	-	-
24	JD	9998	01/10/2015	O/Bal		Opening Balance	0	T9	4,316.00		-	-
25	JD	1001	01/10/2015	O/Bal		Opening Balance	0	T9	7,403.00		-	-
26	JC	9998	01/10/2015	O/Bal		Opening Balance	0	T9		7,403.00	-	-
27	JD	1230	01/10/2015	O/Bal		Opening Balance	0	T9	250.00		-	-
28	JC	9998	01/10/2015	O/Bal		Opening Balance	0	T9		250.00	-	-
29	JD	1200	01/10/2015	O/Bal		Opening Balance	0	T9	10,293.00		-	-
30	JC	9998	01/10/2015	O/Bal		Opening Balance	0	T9		10,293.00	-	-
31	JC	3000	01/10/2015	O/Bal		Opening Balance	0	T9		20,000.00	-	-
32	JD	9998	01/10/2015	O/Bal		Opening Balance	0	T9	20,000.00		-	-

Another important report that you may be required to produce in you UACS assessment is the **Audit Trail**.

This lists every transaction that you have entered on the system. It is from this report that an assessor/marker can track any amendments you may have made to your work when rectifying mistakes. As mentioned at the beginning of this book, you are allowed to make mistakes, as long as you correct them in an appropriate manner. It is therefore vitally important that you print this report accurately.

Firstly, click 'Company' and then 'Financials' (Just as you do to locate the Trial Balance).

From the menu at the top of the screen, select Audit:

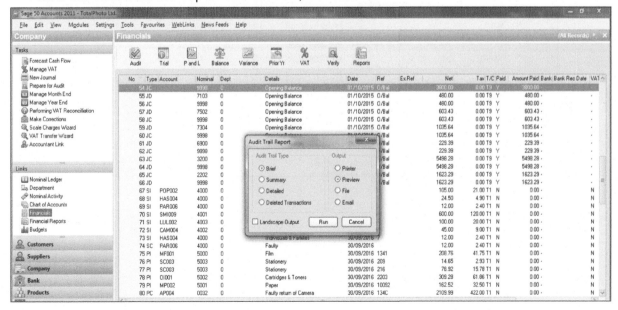

In the assessment, you will be told which report is required, but for this example we are going to select 'Detailed' and then 'Run'.

This screen will then appear:

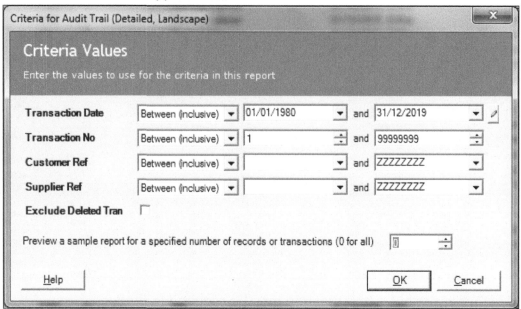

Once you have selected date ranges etc. click ok.

This is how the Audit Trail will look:

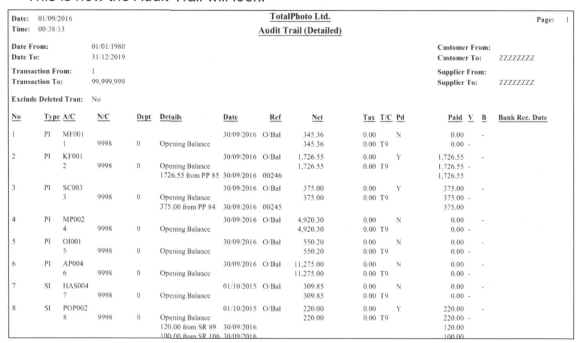

Recurring entries

12

ASSESSMENT CRITERIA

Process recurring receipts and payments (3.2)

CONTENTS

1 Introduction

A company often pays and receives money on a regular basis. For example, it may pay bills monthly or quarterly to organisations for payment such as insurance or rates. Also, it may receive money regularly from customers or other parties, for example receipts for rental income. To make life easier, Sage allows regular payments and receipts to be entered as a '*recurring entry*' which saves the need to process the transaction every month.

2 Creating a new recurring payment

How to process a recurring entry

Click on Bank Current Account via the Bank module and then recurring on the toolbar.

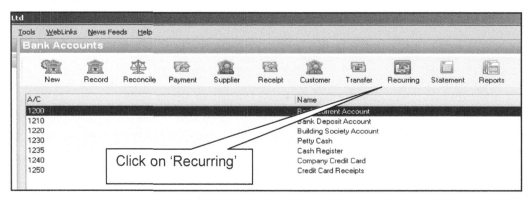

Then click on 'Add' to start entering a new recurring entry. If there are already current recurring entries set up, they will also appear in this screen.

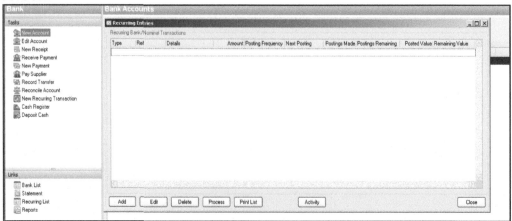

Enter the details for the new recurring entry as shown. These are shown for the following sample direct debit shown in the table below:

Details	Amount	Frequency of payment	No of payments	Payment start date	Payment finish date
Gas	£193.00	Monthly	12	25/6/XX	25/5/XX

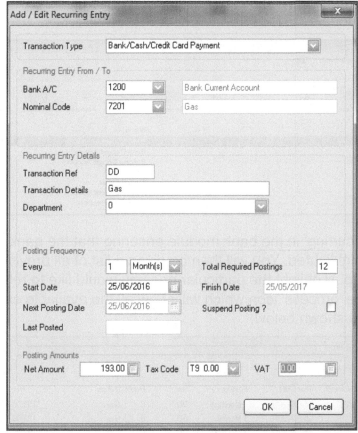

Click OK to save. Once saved the recurring entry will appear in the list as shown:

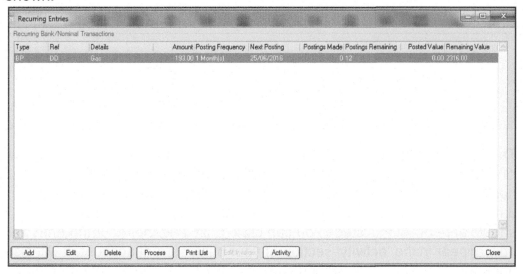

3 Processing a recurring entry for the bank reconciliation process

If a recurring entry has appeared on your bank statement as part of the bank reconciliation process, it will be necessary to 'release' it before you commence the reconciliation itself. This is a very straightforward process and can be done as follows:

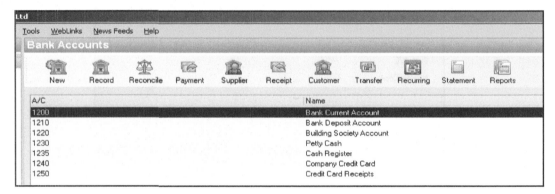

Click on 'Recurring' in the bank module ensuring that the bank current account is highlighted. You will then be given a list of all previous recurring entries set up. Highlight the particular one you would like to release and then click the 'process' icon which will show all the available entries ready to release as shown below:

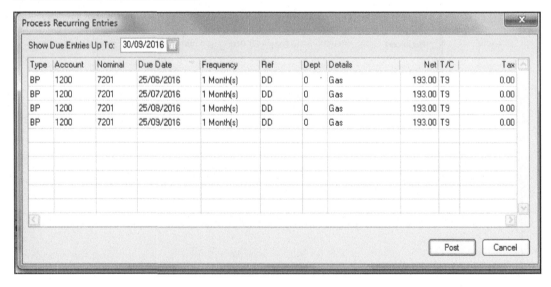

Then type the date of the recurring entry you would like to release in to the 'Show Due Entries Up To' box. This will ensure that you only release the necessary entry to the bank current account. Once you have entered the date click away, anywhere on the screen and the correct transaction should appear. At this stage you can click 'post' and the recurring entry will now appear in the 'activity' section of your bank current account. It will also appear in the list of transactions as part of the bank reconciliation process.

4 Recurring receipts

You are also able to process regular receipts via the recurring entry facility on Sage. This is particularly useful for regular amounts sent to the business such as 'Rent Received'. These types of transactions would be processed in exactly the same way as a Recurring Payment, except the transaction type should be as detailed below within the set up screen:

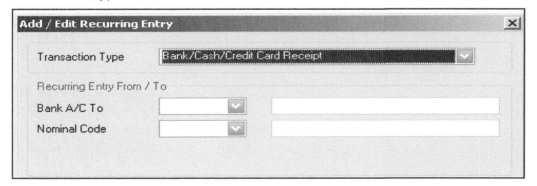

Amending company details and managing data

ASSESSMENT CRITERIA

There are no relevant 'learning outcomes' applicable to this section of the workbook, as the topics covered are not part of the assessment process. However, you are recommend to fully familiarise yourself with all aspects of this chapter.

CONTENTS

1 Amending data

As we have already seen, one of the most common ways to correct an error is by means of a journal. This is essentially a book-keeping solution, using a double entry to correct or amend an earlier error. Sometimes, however, it is necessary to change a transaction we have entered that we cannot correct with a journal.

For example, in the TotalPhoto Case Study we entered a credit note for returned cameras. We cannot enter a journal to correct this as Sage does not allow us to post a journal to a control account (the Creditors Control Account). If we needed to correct this we must go through file maintenance this can be found in File task bar menu:

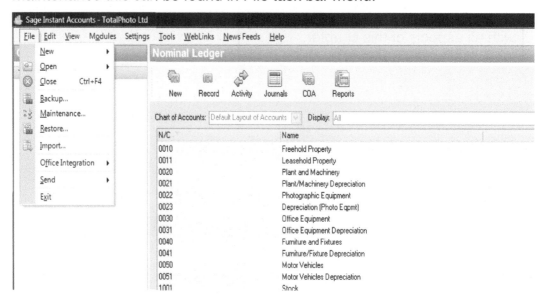

Within file maintenance we have the choice of searching for the item we are trying to correct by many different criteria. One good way to do this is to use the account reference.

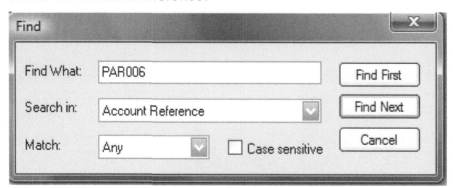

By searching by the account reference of the transaction we are trying to find we can search through the transactions until we find the one we want by clicking [Find Next]

Once we have found the transaction we want we have the choice of either deleting or amending the transaction by clicking the buttons at the top of the screen.

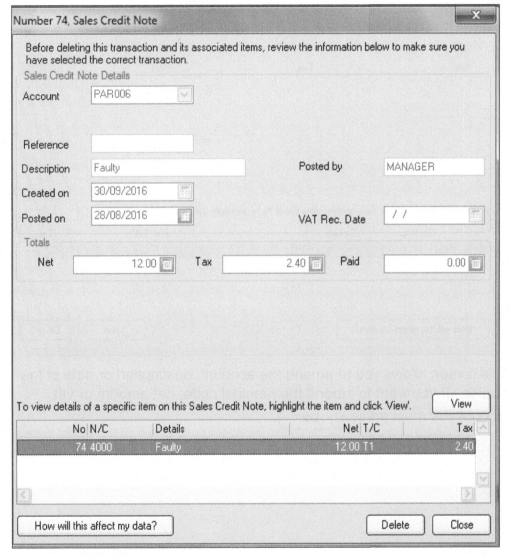

Pressing delete brings up the following screen:

Clicking [Delete] will delete the transaction from the ledger although the fact that it existed will always be shown and it will be offset by a deleting entry as opposed to being completely removed from the ledgers.

Pressing edit brings up the following screen:

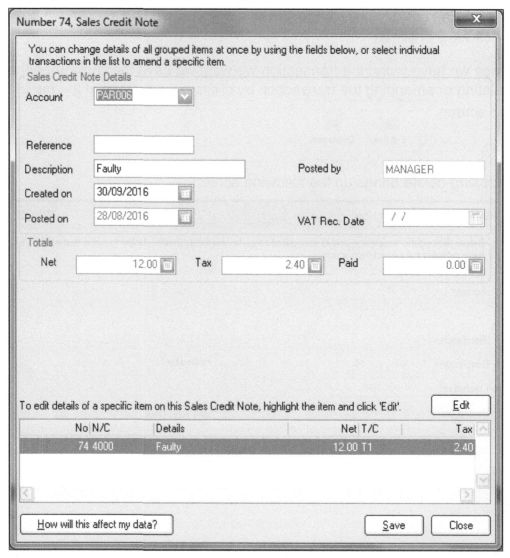

This screen allows you to amend the account, description or date of the invoice. If you want to amend the nominal code, net amount or vat amount you must press Edit.

This brings up this screen:

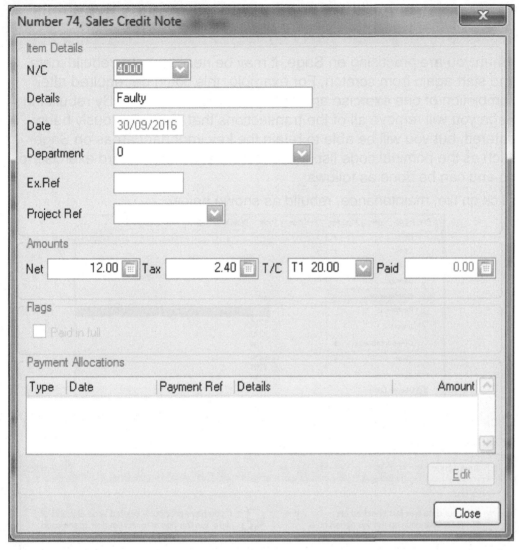

This allows you to amend the nominal code, details, net amount, VAT amount and tax code.

2 Rebuilding and entering new company details

When you are practising on Sage, it may be necessary to 'rebuild' data and start again from scratch. For example, this could be required after completion of one exercise and before starting a new one. By rebuilding Sage you will remove all of the transactions that have previously been entered, but you will be able to retain the key important areas on Sage such as the nominal code list. It is a relatively straightforward exercise to do and can be done as follows:

Click on file, maintenance, rebuild as shown below

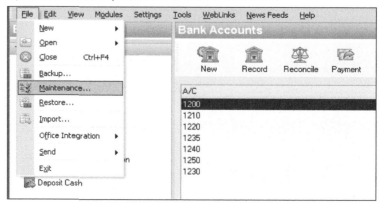

Click rebuild data and then untick all of the boxes shown so that no data is retained.

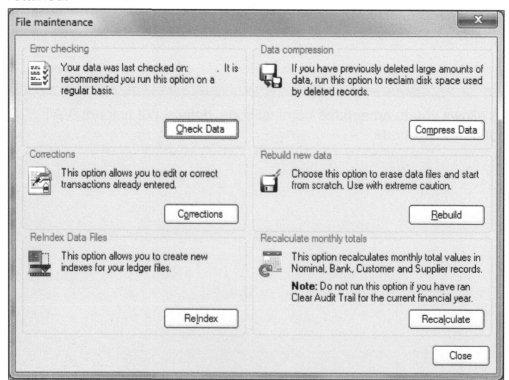

You will then be asked if you would like keep to any transactions, at this stage click '**no**' as shown below:

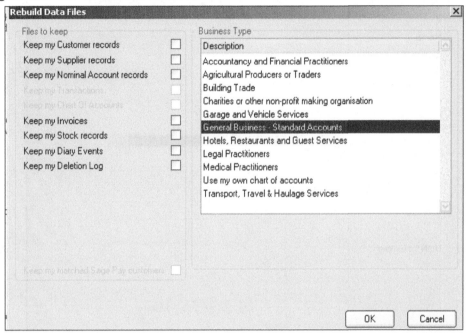

If this was in the workplace you would proceed with extreme caution, but as you are only practising you can rebuild and start again as many times as you wish.

You will be asked what financial year you wish to use for the new data you are using and you can then proceed as normal by entering the company details. A reminder of how this is done is shown below and Sage will display a message to say that all files have been re-built successfully.

The new company's name and address details can be entered by clicking on 'Settings', then 'Company preferences' and the data entry screen for the new company details will appear as shown below:

Important!

Ensure that you set the new 'today's date' as detailed in the new exercise by clicking on '**Settings**' and '**Change Program Date**'. You are now ready to start entering transactions in the normal way.

Processing a returned customer cheque

ASSESSMENT CRITERIA

There are no relevant 'learning outcomes' applicable to this chapter of the Study Text, as the topics covered are not part of the assessment process.

However, you are recommended to fully familiarise yourself with all aspects of this chapter.

CONTENTS

1 Dealing with a returned customer cheque

1 Dealing with a returned customer cheque

There may be time in Sage where you need to correct a transaction, for example, a customer cheque has been returned to you due to insufficient funds (bounced/dishonoured). A returned cheque may not be something that you have to deal with in the live assessment, however, here is how you would deal with this type of transaction on Sage. How you correct a transaction can depend on various different factors, for example, whether it's paid, included in a VAT return or bank reconciled.

When dealing with a returned cheque we need to unallocated the receipt against the invoice.

 Activity

If we refer back to TotalPhoto, let's say that the cheque we received from our customer Lullabies Nursery (LUL002) dated 30th September 2016 was returned due to insufficient funds.

Process this returned cheque through the records and date 30th September 2016. The value of the cheque is £726.90.

To process the returned cheque, you first need to select the customers module and then click on 'Customer write off/refund'. The following screen will appear:

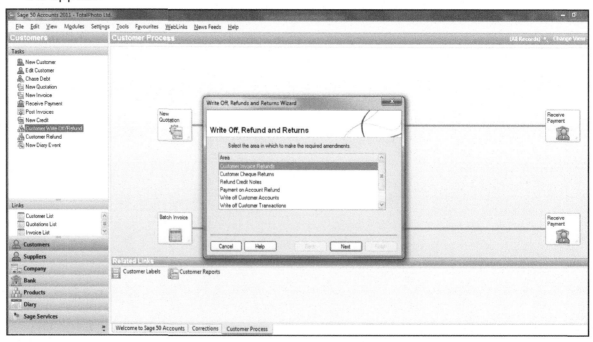

Select 'Customer Cheque Returns' from the list and the following screen will appear:

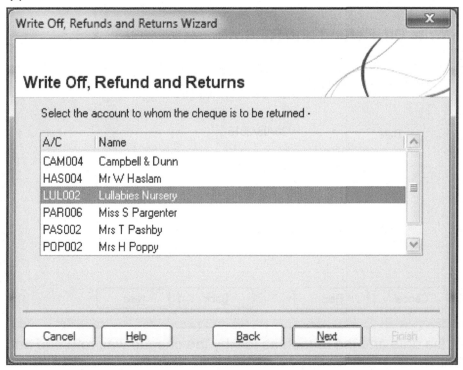

Select the customer for whom a cheque has been returned, in this example it is Lullabies Nursery and then click 'Next'.

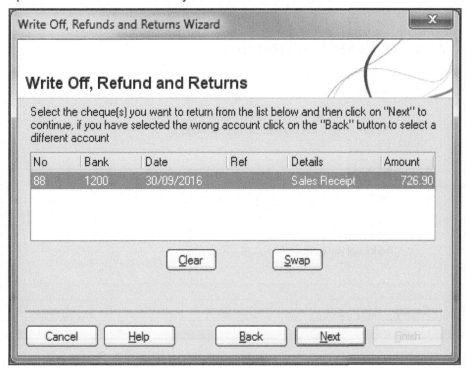

Highlight the cheque that has been returned and click 'Next.

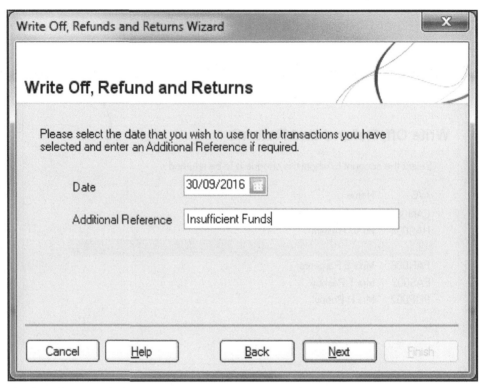

Enter the date and the reason as to why the cheque was returned and click next.

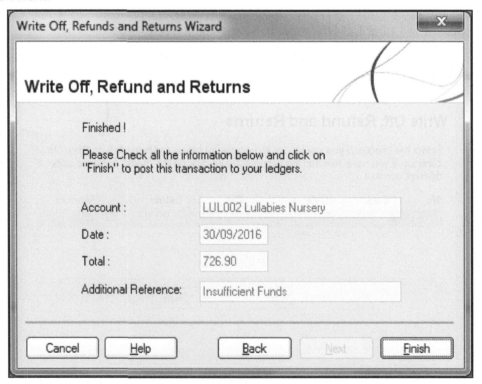

Check all of the details carefully before clicking 'Finish'. Sage will automatically update all of the relevant ledgers in respect of this transaction.

Creating a password to protect data

ASSESSMENT CRITERIA

There are no relevant 'learning outcomes' applicable to this chapter in the Study Text, as the topics covered are not part of the assessment process.

However, you are recommended to fully familiarise yourself with all aspects of this chapter.

CONTENTS

1 Creating a password to protect data

1 Creating a password to protect data

The data entered into the computerised system is sensitive and is open to abuse if not protected effectively. It is a straightforward exercise to protect the data from abuse by creating a password. This password will need to be entered whenever the Sage system is used for the specific company.

How to create a password

Click '**Settings**' and '**Change Password**' as shown in the screen below:

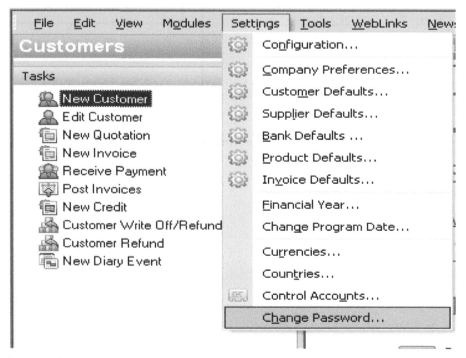

Enter a new password in the '**change password**' box and click **OK** to save.

Your data is now protected and the relevant password will need to be entered whenever access is required to the specific company's data.

PRACTICE ASSESSMENT

1 Practice assessment questions

The situation

This assignment is based on an existing business, Justin Timbercrafts, an organisation that makes small wooden toys which it sells to independent toy stores and the public. The owner of the business is Justin Wilson, who operates as a sole trader.

At the start of business Justin operated a manual book-keeping system, but has now decided that from 1st January 2016, the accounting system will become computerised.

You are employed as an accounting technician in the business.

You can assume that all documentation within this assessment has been checked for accuracy and duly authorised by Justin.

The company details are:

Justin Timbercrafts
27 West Lane
Dornley
DN22 4RD

Sales are to be analysed in four ways:

- The Jungle Collection
- The Farm Collection
- The Pets Collection
- Cash Sales – to members of the public at the small factory shop

The business is registered for VAT (standard scheme) and the rate charged on all items is the basic rate of 20%

All expenditure should be analysed as you feel appropriate.

You should set the system date at 31st January 2016.

The financial year starts in January 2016.

Task 1

Refer to the customer details below and set up customer records to open Sales Ledger Accounts for each customer.

Customer details

Customer Name, Address and Contact Details	Customer Account Code	Customer Account Details
Toyways plc 88 Main Street Longstan LG18 5DF Tel: 01872 628 192 Contact: Brian Mason	TW003	Credit Limit = £5,000 Payment Terms = 30 days Opening Balance = £1,235.76 (relates to invoice 00288 outstanding at 1st January 2016)
Perfect Pastimes Ltd Hubley Industrial Estate Hubley HB29 7FD Tel: 07719 361 281 Contact: Stan Hartley	PP002	Credit Limit = £15,000 Payment Terms = 30 days Opening Balance = £13,209.34 (relates to invoice 00291 outstanding at 1st January 2016)
Happykidz Ltd Churchill Shopping Centre Fearnley FN88 3DS Tel: 07274 792 982 Contact: Shane Humphries	HK006	Credit Limit = £8,000 Payment Terms = 30 days Opening Balance = £342.98 (relates to invoice 00299 outstanding at 1st January 2016)
Prettypops Ltd 10 St Bart's Row Ganningly GN33 2WQ Tel: 0845 198 2828 Contact: Betty Chamberlain	PP004	Credit Limit = £5,000 Payment Terms = 30 days Opening Balance = £190.87 (relates to invoice 00212 outstanding at 1st January 2016)

Task 2

Refer to the Supplier Details below and create supplier records to open Purchase Ledger Accounts for each supplier.

Supplier name, address and contact details	Supplier Account Code	Supplier Account Details
Matchsticks Ltd Unit 66 Haxton HC99 7TG Tel : 02625 389 010 Contact: Amjid Khan	MCS003	Credit Limit = £5000 Payment Terms = 30 days Opening Balance = £1943.26 (relates to Invoice 2033 outstanding at 1st January 2016)
Willow Works Ltd Ceder House Lanchester LN33 7DK Tel: 07727 373 7281 Contact: Hin Lan Hun	WWW002	Credit Limit = £8,500 Payment Terms= 30 days Opening Balance = £288.29 (relates to Invoice 38842 outstanding at 1st January 2016)
Grange Toys Ltd The Lodge Kilminster KG18 6GC Tel : 0845 283 1298 Contact: Jake Newlove	GRT005	Credit Limit = £10,000 Payment Terms = 30 days Opening Balance = £4,277.50 (relates to Invoice GT2640 outstanding at 1st January 2016)
FLW Ltd 199 Duncan Avenue Hurtleby HB28 4FS Tel : 07227 290 3832 Contact: Emma Rose	FLW002	Credit Limit = £3,000 Payment Terms = 14 days Opening Balance = £923.46 (relates to Invoice 2727 outstanding at 1st January 2016)
Dornley Evening Chronicle 11 Dundee Street Dornley DN22 6FD Tel : 01822 281 881 Contact: Holly Maclay	DEC004	Credit Limit = £1,000 Payment Terms = 30 days Opening Balance = £0.00

Task 3.1

Create new, or amend the following nominal codes

Account number	Account name
4000	Sales – Jungle Collection
4001	Sales – Farm Collection
4002	Sales – Pets Collection
4003	Cash Sales
3260	Drawings
7100	Rent and Rates

Task 3.2

Refer to the list of nominal ledger balances below. Enter the opening balances onto the computerised accounting system, making sure you select the appropriate nominal ledger codes.

List of general ledger balances as at the 1st January 2016.

Account Name	£ DR	£ CR
Motor Vehicles	4,586.00	
IT Equipment	3684.00	
Bank Current Account	11,203.30	
Petty Cash	150.00	
Sales Ledger Control Account*	14978.95	
Purchase Ledger Control Account*		7432.51
Sales – Jungle Collection		17,293.50
Sales – Farm Collection		19,224.70
Sales – Pets Collection		10,260.45
Cash Sales		5,431.40
Capital		20,000.00
Rent and Rates	2,400.00	
Insurance	720.00	
Advertising	1,420.00	
Cost of Sales - Materials	28,344.80	
Office Costs	2,350.00	
Miscellaneous Motor Expenses	9805.51	
*You do not need to enter these figures as you have already entered opening balances for customers and suppliers	79,642.56	79,642.56

Task 3.3

Transfer £1000.00 from the bank current account to the bank deposit account. Enter this on to the computerised accounting system using reference TRF01 dated 1st January 2016.

Task 3.4

Print out the following reports and **identify and correct any errors**:

- Customer Address List
- Supplier address List
- Period Trial Balance Report

Task 4

You have received the following e-mail from FLW Ltd (a supplier). Enter the new address and telephone number into the accounting system.

To:	accounts@justintimbercrafts.co.uk
From:	emmarose@networks.com
Date:	29/12/2016

Hi there

Just to let you know that we are moving! From 31st December our new address will be Emsley House, Radleigh, RD77 3ED.

Our new phone number is 01442 737 321.

Please ensure that you update all records with this change in address.

Kind regards,

Emma

Task 5

Enter the following sales invoices and credit note onto the computerised accounting system.

Justin Timbercrafts
27 West Lane
Dornley
DN22 4RD
"Quality Wooden Toys at Affordable Prices"

INVOICE 00300
Tax Point : 2nd January 2016   VAT Registration Number: 4839101298

Happykidz Ltd
Churchill Shopping Centre
Fearnley
FN88 3DS

Farm Collections × 8	£7.00	£56.00
Jungle Collections × 10	£9.00	£90.00
		£146.00
VAT @ 20.0%		£29.20
TOTAL FOR PAYMENT		£175.20

Terms: 30 days

Justin Timbercrafts
27 West Lane
Dornley
DN22 4RD
"Quality Wooden Toys at Affordable Prices"

INVOICE 00301
Tax Point : 2nd January 2016   VAT Registration Number: 4839101298

Toyways plc
88 Main Street
Longstan
LG18 5DF

Farm Collections × 5	£7.00	£35.00
Jungle Collections × 5	£9.00	£45.00
Pets Collections × 5	£9.00	£45.00
		£125.00
VAT @ 20.0%		£25.00
TOTAL FOR PAYMENT		£150.00

Terms: 30 days

Justin Timbercrafts
27 West Lane
Dornley
DN22 4RD
"Quality Wooden Toys at Affordable Prices"

INVOICE 00302
Tax Point : 4th January 2016   VAT Registration Number: 4839101298

Happykidz Ltd
Churchill Shopping Centre
Fearnley
FN88 3DS

Farm Collections × 4	£7.00	£28.00
Pets Collections × 8	£9.00	£72.00
		£100.00
VAT @ 20.0%		£20.00
TOTAL FOR PAYMENT		£120.00

Terms: 30 days

Justin Timbercrafts
27 West Lane
Dornley
DN22 4RD
"Quality Wooden Toys at Affordable Prices"

CREDIT NOTE 55
Tax Point : 2nd January 2016   VAT Registration Number: 4839101298

Happykidz Ltd
Churchill Shopping Centre
Fearnley
FN88 3DS

Farm Collections × 2 (Broken)	£7.00	£14.00
VAT @ 20.0%		£2.80
TOTAL FOR PAYMENT		£16.80

Terms: 30 days

Task 6

Enter the following purchases invoices onto the computer system.

Date	Supplier	Invoice No	Gross £	VAT £	Net £	Materials	Advertising
2/1/16	Dornley Evening Chronicle	2929/11	156.00	26.00	130.00		130.00
3/1/16	Grange Toys Ltd	GT2882	1,272.00	212.00	1,060.00	1,060.00	
6/1/16	Willow Works Ltd	99128	288.00	48.00	240.00	240.00	
	Totals		**1,716.00**	**286.00**	**1,430.00**	**1,300.00**	**130.00**

Task 7

Refer to the following summary of payments received from customers and made to suppliers. Enter the receipts and payments into the computer, making sure you allocate all amounts as shown in the details column.

Cheque / BACS Receipts Listing

Date	Details	Customer	£	How Received
03 Jan 16	Payment of opening balance	Toyways plc	1235.76	Cheque
05 Jan 16	Payment of opening balance	Happykidz Ltd	342.98	BACS

Cheques Paid Listing

Date	Details	Supplier	£	Cheque Number
04 Jan 16	Payment of opening balance	FLW Ltd	923.46	0012671
04 Jan 16	Payment of opening balance	Matchsticks Ltd	1943.26	0012672

Task 8

Refer to the following email from Justin:

email
From : Justin@justintimbercrafts.co.uk
To : accounts@justintimbercrafts.co.uk
Date: 5 January 2016
Subject: Prettypops Ltd
Hi
I'm afraid that Prettypops Ltd have gone into liquidation – I've just had a letter from their administrators. It looks most unlikely we will get anything for their outstanding account – which stands at £190.87.
Please write this amount off as a bad debt.
Thanks
Justin

Print a new customer statement showing the amount written off and the new balance of NIL. Treat using no VAT.

Task 9

Enter the following petty cash payments into the computerised system:-

Petty Cash Voucher	
Voucher no 10	
Date 3 January 2016	
Details	
Window cleaner (*zero rated for VAT purposes*) Receipt attached	£20.00

Petty Cash Voucher	
Voucher no 11	
Date 5 January 2016	
Details	
5 × New calculators	£20.00
VAT	£4.00
Total	£24.00
Receipt attached	

Task 10

Refer to the following cash sales and enter receipts into the computer. Use the bank current account for this transaction and enter 'cash sales' as the reference.

Date	Receipt type	Gross	VAT	NET	Nominal code
2nd Jan	Cash sale	78.24	13.04	65.20	4003
4th Jan	Cash sale	102.30	17.05	85.25	4003

Task 11

Enter the following journal onto the computerised accounting system.

Reference: JNL01			
Date	**Account Name & Code**	**Dr**	**Cr**
25/1/16	Drawings	200.00	
	Bank Current Account		200.00
Being the transfer of cash for Justin Wilson's personal use.			

Task 12

Refer to the following email from Justin:

email
From : Justin@justintimbercrafts.co.uk
To : accounts@justintimbercrafts.co.uk
Date: 6 January 2016
Subject: Opening Balances

Could you please enter the details of a new customer that I have agreed terms with this morning? You will need to set up a new customer record for them with an opening balance of nil.

The details are:

Funnystuff Ltd
31 Yew Tree Way
Hedgefield
HD43 2WA

Contact: James Strong

The settlement terms are 30 days with a credit limit of £1,000.

Please use account code FS001 for this customer

Thanks

Justin

Task 13

Once you have opened up a new customer record for Funnystuff, print a screen shot of the new customer's record card showing the name and address details. Refer to the following sales invoice for the new customer Funnystuff Ltd, and existing customer Toyways Plc. Enter the two invoices (detailed on the following page) onto the computer system.

Justin Timbercrafts
27 West Lane
Dornley
DN22 4RD
"Quality Wooden Toys at Affordable Prices"

INVOICE 00303
Tax Point : 6th January 2016   VAT Registration Number: 4839101298

Funnystuff Ltd
31 Yew Tree Way
Hedgefield
HD43 2WA

Farm Collections × 5	£7.00	£35.00
Pets Collections × 5	£9.00	£45.00
		£80.00
VAT @ 20.0%		£16.00
TOTAL FOR PAYMENT		£96.00

Terms: 30 days

Justin Timbercrafts
27 West Lane
Dornley
DN22 4RD
"Quality Wooden Toys at Affordable Prices"

INVOICE 00304
Tax Point : 6th January 2016   VAT Registration Number: 4839101298

Toyways plc
88 Main Street
Longstan
LG18 5DF

Pets Collections × 30	£9.00	£270.00
VAT @ 20.0%		£54.00
TOTAL FOR PAYMENT		£324.00

Terms: 30 days

Task 14

Enter the following purchase invoices into the computer system.

Date	Supplier Name	Invoice Number	Gross £	VAT £	Net £	Materials £	Advertising £
8/1/16	Matchsticks Ltd	3178	1680.00	280.00	1400.00	1400.00	
10/1/16	Grange Toys Ltd	GT2916	672.00	112.00	560.00	560.00	
		Total	2352.00	392.00	1960.00	1960.00	

Task 15

Refer to the following summary of payments received from customers and made to suppliers. Enter the receipts and payments into the bank current account, making sure you allocate all amounts as shown in the details column.

Cheque / BACS Receipts Listing

Date	Details	Customer	£	How Received
11/1/16	Payment of Invoice 00300 including credit note CN55	Happykidz Ltd	158.40	BACS

Cheques Paid Listing

Date	Details	Supplier	£	Cheque Number
11/1/16	Payment of opening balance	Willow Works Ltd	288.29	0012674
14/1/16	Part-payment of opening balance	Grange Toys Ltd	3000.00	0012675
14/1/16	Payment of Invoice 2929/11	Dornley Evening Chronicle	156.00	0012676

Task 16

Refer to the following petty cash vouchers and enter into the computerised system:

Petty Cash Voucher

Voucher 12

Date 12 January 2016

Details	
Train fare – exempt for VAT	£14.80
Receipt attached	

Petty Cash Voucher

Voucher 13

Date 14 January 2016

Details	
Photocopy paper	£8.50
VAT	£1.70
Total	£10.20
Receipt attached	

Task 17

Refer to the following e-mail from Justin:

---

email

From : Justin@justintimbercrafts.co.uk

To : accounts@justintimbercrafts.co.uk

Date: 14 January 2016

Subject: Bank Loan

Hi

I don't know if you remember me telling you but I applied for a business loan of £10,000.00 a few weeks ago. This has been granted and has been received into the bank current account today. Please can you ensure that you enter this into the computer system.

Thanks

Justin

Enter the following journal to record the receipt of the above bank loan.

Reference: JNL02			
Date	**Account Name & Code**	**Dr**	**Cr**
14/1/16	Bank Current Account	10000.00	
	Loan		10000.00
Being the receipt of loan proceeds.			

Task 18

Refer to the following receipt for the purchase of a new picture, paid for by petty cash. Use voucher code 14 for this transaction. This is a picture for the office wall, so should be coded to 'Office Stationery'.

Receipt Number 1289

Art of the Matter

Kitchener Shopping Centre

Miltonby

VAT Reg: 343 4839 47

Date : 14 January 2016

Received from Justin Timbercrafts, by cash, for original print

£25 inc VAT

Task 19

Refer to the following schedule of standing orders. You need to set these up as recurring payments on the computer system. Both of the payments should be set up exempt of VAT.

1   Set up a recurring entry for each transaction as shown in the standing order schedule below.

2   Print a screen shot of the screen setting up the recurring entries.

3   Process the first payment for each one.

Details	Amount	Frequency	Total payments	Payment start date	Payment finish date
P Smith (Rent)	£400	Monthly	12	18 January 2016	18 December 2016

Details	Amount	Frequency	Total payments	Payment start date	Payment finish date
Dornley Council (Rates)	£120.00	Monthly	12	28 January 2016	28 December 2016

Task 20

Process the following journal. The sum of £150.00 for insurance costs have been incorrectly posted to the Gas account in error. Enter the following journal to correct the error using reference no:

Journal – 20 January 2016		
Ref : JNL03	Dr £	Cr £
Insurance	150.00	
Gas		150.00
Being correction of error recording insurance as gas costs		

Task 21

Refer to the email below from Justin:

email
From : Justin@justintimbercrafts.co.uk
To : accounts@justintimbercrafts.co.uk
Date: 31st January 2016
Subject: Petty cash
Hi Please transfer £94.00 from the bank account to the petty cash account to reimburse the petty cash float – this should reinstate it to £150.00. Use reference TRFO2 for this transaction. Thanks Justin

Task 22

An office printer has been purchased for £250.00 including VAT. This was paid for via the bank current account (cheque no 0012673 on 9/1/2016). Process this payment on the computer system (IT Equipment 0030).

Task 23

You are given the following bank statement and are asked to produce a bank reconciliation as at 31 January 2016, processing any adjustments that may be necessary. Enter the bank charges (no VAT) which have not yet been accounted for. Reconcile the bank statement.

MIDWEST BANK plc
109 Church Street
Dornley
DN12 5DE

Justin Timbercrafts
27 West Lane
Dornley
DN22 4RD

Account Number : 341723810

31 January 2016

Statement of Account – Sheet 819

Date	Details	Paid out £	Paid in £	Balance £
1 August	Opening Balance			11203.30 Cr
01/01/2016	Transfer	1000.00		10203.30 Cr
02/01/2016	Counter credit		78.24	10281.54 Cr
04/01/2016	Counter credit		102.30	10383.84 Cr
05/01/2016	BGC		1235.76	11619.60 Cr
05/01/2016	BACS Receipt		342.98	11962.58 Cr
10/01/2016	Chq 0012671	923.46		11039.12 Cr
11/01/2016	BACS receipt		158.40	11197.52 Cr
12/01/2016	Chq 0012672	1943.26		9254.26 Cr
12/01/2016	Chq 0012673	250.00		9004.26 Cr
14/01/2016	Loan proceeds		10000.00	19004.26 Cr
15/01/2016	Chq 0012675	3000.00		16004.26 Cr
15/01/2016	Direct Debit	400.00		15604.26 Cr
16/01/2016	Direct Debit	120.00		15484.26 Cr
25/01/2016	Counter debit	200.00		15284.26 Cr
28/01/2016	Bank Charges	32.00		15252.26 Cr
31/01/2016	Counter credit	94.00		15158.26 Cr
31/01/2016	Closing Balance			15158.26 Cr

CR = Credit
DR = Debit

Task 24

Print the following reports

- Customer Activity (detailed) report

- Supplier Activity (detailed) report

- Period Trial Balance for the month of August

- Audit Trail for August (detailed – transactions only)

- Aged payables report (summary)

- Aged receivables report (summary)

- Nominal Ledger Activity Report for the following accounts

    (a) Bank Current Account

    (b) Petty Cash Account

- Journal Day Book

- Bank Statement

PRACTICE ASSESSMENT ANSWERS

KAPLAN PUBLISHING

2 Practice assessment answers

Task 3.4

Customer Address List

Date:	29/08/2016	Justin Timbercrafts		Page:	1
Time:	19:59:37	Customer Address List			

Customer From:
Customer To: ZZZZZZZ

A/C	Name & Address	Contact Name	Telephone	Fax
HK006	Happykidz Ltd Churchill Shopping Centre Fearnley FN88 3DS	Shane Humphries	07274 792 982	
PP002	Perfect Pastimes Ltd Hubley Industrial Estate Hubley HB29 7FD	Stan Hartley	07719 361 281	
PP004	Prettypops Ltd. 10 St Bart's Row Canningly GN33 2WQ	Betty Chamberlain	0845 198 2828	
TW003	Toyways Plc 88 Main Street Longstan LG18 5DF	Brian Mason	01872 628 192	

Supplier Address List

Date:	29/08/2016	**Justin Timbercrafts**		Page:	1
Time:	20:02:36	**Supplier Address List**			

Supplier From:
Supplier To: ZZZZZZZZ

A/C	Name	Contact	Telephone	Fax
DEC004	Dornley Evening Chronicle 11 Dundee Street Dornley DN22 6FD	Holly Maclay	01822 281 881	
FLW002	FLW Ltd 199 Duncan Avenue Hurtleby HB28 4FS	Emma Rose	07227 290 383	
GRT005	Grange Toys Ltd. The Lodge Kilminster KG18 6GC	Jake Newlove	0845 283 1298	
MCS003	Matchsticks Ltd. Unit 66 Haxton HC99 7TG	Amjid Khan	02625 389 010	
WWW002	Willow Works Ltd Cedar House Lanchester LN33 7DK	Hin Lan Hun	07727 373 728	

Trial Balance

Date:	29/08/2016	**Justin Timbercrafts**		Page:	1
Time:	20:04:18	**Period Trial Balance**			

To Period: Month 12, December 2016

N/C	Name	Debit	Credit
0030	IT Equipment	3,684.00	
0050	Motor Vehicles	4,586.00	
1100	Sales Ledger Control Account	14,978.95	
1200	Bank Current Account	10,203.30	
1210	Bank Deposit Account	1,000.00	
1230	Petty Cash	150.00	
2100	Purchase Ledger Control Account		7,432.51
3000	Capital		20,000.00
4000	Sales - Jungle Farm Collection		17,293.50
4001	Sales - Farm Collection		19,224.70
4002	Sales - Pets Collection		10,260.45
4003	Cash Sales		5,431.40
5000	Purchases of Materials	28,344.80	
6201	Advertising	1,420.00	
7100	Rent and Rates	2,400.00	
7104	Insurance	720.00	
7304	Miscellaneous Motor Expenses	9,805.51	
7504	Office Stationery	2,350.00	
	Totals:	79,642.56	79,642.56

Task 8

Customer Statement

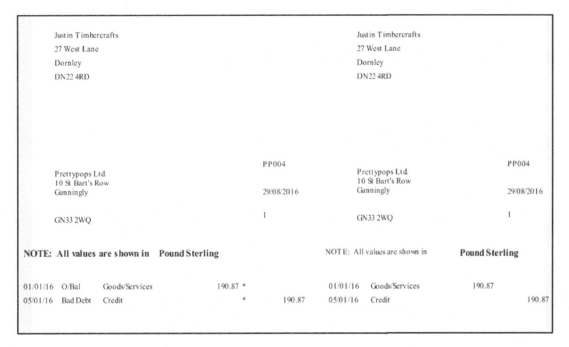

Task 13

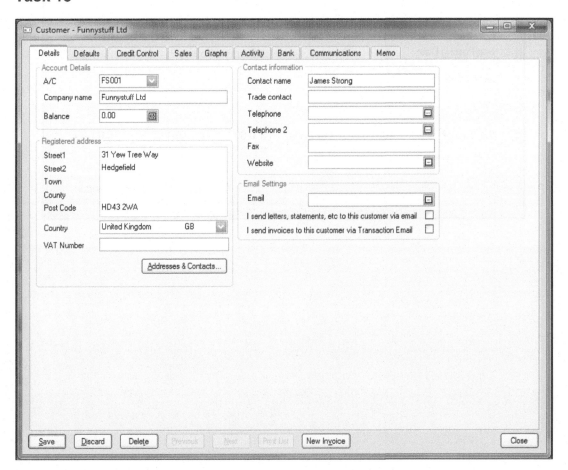

Task 19 – Setting up recurring entries and processing the first payments

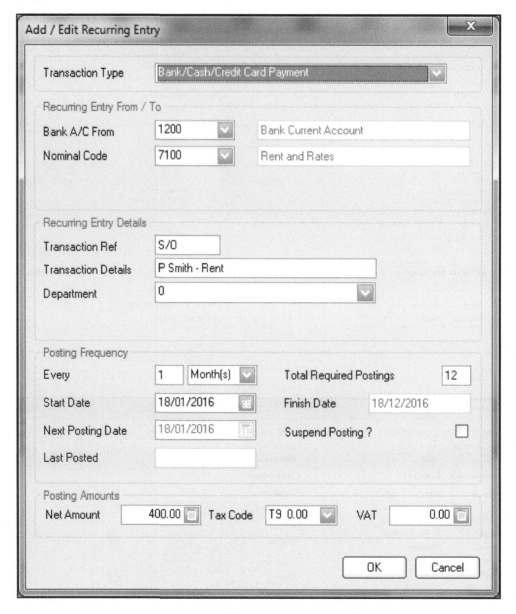

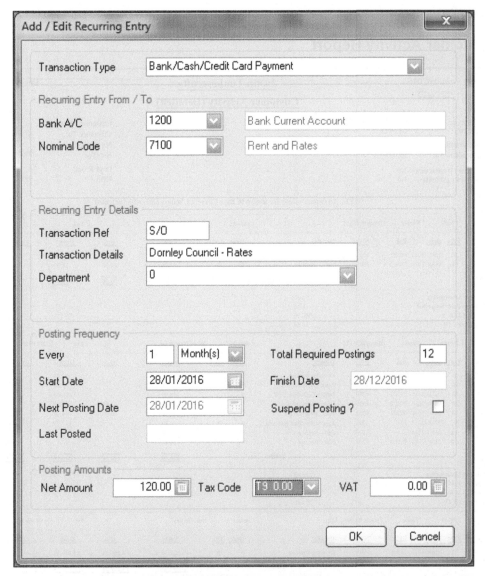

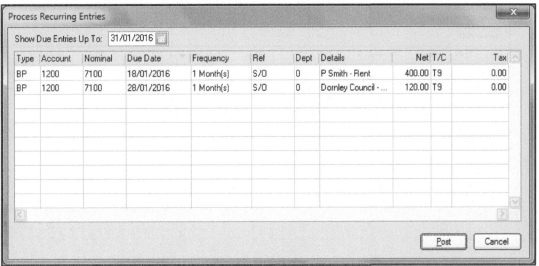

Task 24

Customer Activity Report

Date:	04/09/2016				**Justin Timbercrafts**						Page:	1	
Time:	22:26:12				**Customer Activity (Detailed)**								

Date From:	01/01/1980								Customer From:				
Date To:	04/09/2016								Customer To:	ZZZZZZZZ			
Transaction From:	1								N/C From:				
Transaction To:	99,999,999								N/C To:	99999999			
Inc b/fwd transaction:	No								Dept From:	0			
Exc later payment:	No								Dept To:	999			

** NOTE: All report values are shown in Base Currency, unless otherwise indicated **

A/C:	FS001	Name:	Funnystuff Ltd				Contact:	James Strong			Tel:			

No	Type	Date	Ref	N/C	Details	Dept	T/C	Value	O/S	Debit	Credit	V	B
25	SI	06/01/2016	00303	4001	Farm Collection x 5	0	T1	42.00 *	42.00	42.00		N	-
26	SI	06/01/2016	00303	4002	Pets Collection x 5	0	T1	54.00 *	54.00	54.00		N	-
					Totals:			96.00	96.00	96.00			

Amount Outstanding	96.00
Amount Paid this period	0.00
Credit Limit £	1,000.00
Turnover YTD	80.00

A/C:	HK006	Name:	Happykidz Ltd				Contact:	Shane Humphries			Tel:	07274 792982		

No	Type	Date	Ref	N/C	Details	Dept	T/C	Value	O/S	Debit	Credit	V	B
3	SI	01/01/2016	O/Bal	9998	Opening Balance	0	T9	342.98		342.98			
9	SI	02/01/2016	00300	4001	Farm Collection x 8	0	T1	67.20		67.20		N	-
10	SI	02/01/2016	00300	4000	Jungle Collection x 10	0	T1	108.00		108.00		N	-
14	SI	04/01/2016	00302	4001	Farm Collection x 4	0	T1	33.60 *	33.60	33.60		N	-
15	SI	04/01/2016	00302	4002	Pets Collection x 8	0	T1	86.40 *	86.40	86.40		N	-
16	SC	02/01/2016	55	4001	Farm collections (broken)	0	T1	16.80			16.80	N	-
21	SR	05/01/2016		1200	Sales Receipt	0	T9	342.98			342.98	-	N
30	SR	11/01/2016	BACS	1200	Sales Receipt	0	T9	158.40			158.40	-	N
					Totals:			120.00	120.00	638.18	518.18		

Amount Outstanding	120.00
Amount Paid this period	501.38
Credit Limit £	8,000.00
Turnover YTD	574.98

A/C:	PP002	Name:	Perfect Pastimes Ltd				Contact:	Stan Hartley			Tel:	07719 361281		

No	Type	Date	Ref	N/C	Details	Dept	T/C	Value	O/S	Debit	Credit	V	B
2	SI	01/01/2016	O/Bal	9998	Opening Balance	0	T9	13,209.34 *	13,209.34	13,209.34		-	-
					Totals:			13,209.34	13,209.34	13,209.34			

Amount Outstanding	13,209.34
Amount Paid this period	0.00
Credit Limit £	15,000.00
Turnover YTD	13,209.34

A/C:	PP004	Name:	Prettypops Ltd				Contact:	Betty Chamberlain			Tel:	0845 1982828		

No	Type	Date	Ref	N/C	Details	Dept	T/C	Value	O/S	Debit	Credit	V	B
4	SI	01/01/2016	O/Bal	9998	Opening Balance	0	T9	190.87		190.87		-	-
24	SC	05/01/2016	BADDBT	8100	Bad Debt Write Off	0	T9	190.87			190.87	-	-
					Totals:			0.00	0.00	190.87	190.87		

Amount Outstanding	0.00
Amount Paid this period	0.00
Credit Limit £	5,000.00
Turnover YTD	190.87

Date:	04/09/2016				**Justin Timbercrafts**						Page:	2	
Time:	22:26:12				**Customer Activity (Detailed)**								

A/C:	TW003	Name:	Toyways Ltd		Contact:		Brian Mason		Tel:	01872 628192		

No	Type	Date	Ref	N/C	Details	Dept	T/C	Value	O/S	Debit	Credit	V	B
1	SI	01/01/2016	O/Bal	9998	Opening Balance	0	T9	1,235.76		1,235.76		-	-
11	SI	02/01/2016	00301	4001	Farm Collecton x 5	0	T1	42.00 *	42.00	42.00		N	-
12	SI	02/01/2016	00301	4000	Jungle Collection x 5	0	T1	54.00 *	54.00	54.00		N	-
13	SI	02/01/2016	00301	4002	Pets Collection x 5	0	T1	54.00 *	54.00	54.00		N	-
20	SR	03/01/2016		1200	Sales Receipt	0	T9	1,235.76			1,235.76	-	N
27	SI	06/01/2016	00304	4002	Pets Collection x 30	0	T1	324.00 *	324.00	324.00		N	-
					Totals:			474.00	474.00	1,709.76	1,235.76		

Amount Outstanding	474.00
Amount Paid this period	1,235.76
Credit Limit £	5,000.00
Turnover YTD	1,630.76

Supplier Activity Report

Date:	04/09/2016			**Justin Timbercrafts**					Page:	1
Time:	22:26:55			**Supplier Activity (Detailed)**						

Date From:	01/01/1980					Supplier From:	
Date To:	04/09/2016					Supplier To:	ZZZZZZZZ
Transaction From:	1					N/C From:	
Transaction To:	99,999,999					N/C To:	99999999
Inc b/fwd transaction:	No					Dept From:	0
Exc later payment:	No					Dept To:	999

** NOTE: All report values are shown in Base Currency, unless otherwise indicated **

A/C:	DEC004	Name:	Dornley Evening Chronicle			Contact:	Holly Maclay		Tel:	01822 281881

No	Type	Date	Ref	N/C	Details	Dept	T/C	Value	O/S	Debit	Credit	V	B
17	PI	02/01/2016	2929/11	6201	Advertising	0	T1	156.00	0.00		156.00	N	-
33	PP	14/01/2016	0012676	1200	Purchase Payment	0	T9	156.00	0.00	156.00		-	N
					Totals:			0.00	0.00	156.00	156.00		

Amount Outstanding	0.00
Amount paid this period	156.00
Credit Limit £	1,000.00
Turnover YTD	130.00

A/C:	FLW002	Name:	FLW Ltd			Contact:	Emma Rose		Tel:	07227 290383

No	Type	Date	Ref	N/C	Details	Dept	T/C	Value	O/S	Debit	Credit	V	B
8	PI	01/01/2016	O/Bal	9998	Opening Balance	0	T9	923.46	0.00		923.46	-	-
22	PP	04/01/2016	0012671	1200	Purchase Payment	0	T9	923.46	0.00	923.46		-	N
					Totals:			0.00	0.00	923.46	923.46		

Amount Outstanding	0.00
Amount paid this period	923.46
Credit Limit £	3,000.00
Turnover YTD	923.46

A/C:	GRT005	Name:	Grange Toys Ltd			Contact:	Jake Newlove		Tel:	0845 2831298

No	Type	Date	Ref	N/C	Details	Dept	T/C	Value	O/S	Debit	Credit	V	B
7	PI	01/01/2016	O/Bal	9998	Opening Balance	0	T9	4,277.50 p	1,277.50		4,277.50	-	-
18	PI	03/01/2016	GT2882	5000	Materials	0	T1	1,272.00 *	1,272.00		1,272.00	N	-
29	PI	11/01/2016	GT2916	5000	Materials	0	T1	672.00 *	672.00		672.00	N	-
32	PP	14/01/2016	0012675	1200	Purchase Payment	0	T9	3,000.00	0.00	3,000.00		-	N
					Totals:			3,221.50	3,221.50	3,000.00	6,221.50		

Amount Outstanding	3,221.50
Amount paid this period	3,000.00
Credit Limit £	10,000.00
Turnover YTD	5,897.50

A/C:	MCS003	Name:	Matchsticks Ltd			Contact:	Amjid Khan		Tel:	02625 389010

No	Type	Date	Ref	N/C	Details	Dept	T/C	Value	O/S	Debit	Credit	V	B
5	PI	01/01/2016	O/Bal	9998	Opening Balance	0	T9	1,943.26	0.00		1,943.26	-	-
23	PP	04/01/2016	0012672	1200	Purchase Payment	0	T9	1,943.26	0.00	1,943.26		-	N
28	PI	08/01/2016	3178	5000	Materials	0	T1	1,680.00 *	1,680.00		1,680.00	N	-
					Totals:			1,680.00	1,680.00	1,943.26	3,623.26		

Amount Outstanding	1,680.00
Amount paid this period	1,943.26
Credit Limit £	5,000.00
Turnover YTD	3,343.26

Date:	04/09/2016						Justin Timbercrafts			Page:	2	
Time:	22:26:55						Supplier Activity (Detailed)					

A/C:	WWW002	Name:		Willow Works Ltd			Contact:		Hin Lan Hun			Tel:		07727 373728		

No	Type	Date	Ref	N/C	Details	Dept	T/C	Value	O/S	Debit	Credit	V	B
6	PI	01/01/2016	O/Bal	9998	Opening Balance	0	T9	288.29	0.00		288.29	·	·
19	PI	06/01/2016	99128	5000	Materials	0	T1	288.00 *	288.00		288.00	N	·
31	PP	11/01/2016	0012674	1200	Purchase Payment	0	T9	288.29	0.00	288.29		·	N
					Totals:			288.00	288.00	288.29	576.29		

Amount Outstanding	288.00
Amount paid this period	288.29
Credit Limit £	8,500.00
Turnover YTD	528.29

Period Trial Balance for January

Date:	29/08/2016		Justin Timbercrafts	Page:	1
Time:	20:59:50		Period Trial Balance		

To Period: Month 1, January 2016

N/C	Name	Debit	Credit
0030	IT Equipment	3,892.33	
0050	Motor Vehicles	4,586.00	
1100	Sales Ledger Control Account	13,899.34	
1200	Bank Current Account	14,713.97	
1210	Bank Deposit Account	1,000.00	
1230	Petty Cash	175.00	
2100	Purchase Ledger Control Account		5,189.50
2200	Sales Tax Control Account		171.49
2201	Purchase Tax Control Account	725.37	
2300	Loans		10,000.00
3000	Capital		20,000.00
3260	Drawings	200.00	
4000	Sales - Jungle Farm Collection		17,428.50
4001	Sales - Farm Collection		19,364.70
4002	Sales - Pets Collection		10,692.45
4003	Cash Sales		5,581.85
5000	Purchases of Materials	31,604.80	
6201	Advertising	1,550.00	
7100	Rent and Rates	2,920.00	
7104	Insurance	870.00	
7201	Gas		150.00
7304	Miscellaneous Motor Expenses	9,805.51	
7400	Travelling	14.80	
7504	Office Stationery	2,378.50	
7801	Cleaning	20.00	
7901	Bank Charges	32.00	
8100	Bad Debt Write Off	190.87	
	Totals:	88,578.49	88,578.49

Audit Trail

| Date: | 29/08/2016 | | | | | **Justin Timbercrafts** | | | | | | | | Page: | 1 |
| Time: | 21:01:38 | | | | | **Audit Trail (Detailed)** | | | | | | | | | |

Date From:	01/01/1980										Customer From:			
Date To:	31/01/2016										Customer To:	ZZZZZZZZ		
Transaction From:	1										Supplier From:			
Transaction To:	99,999,999										Supplier To:	ZZZZZZZZ		
Exclude Deleted Tran:	No													

No	Type	A/C	N/C	Dept	Details	Date	Ref	Net	Tax	T/C	Pd	Paid	V	B	Bank Rec. Date
1	SI	TW003				01/01/2016	O/Bal	1,235.76	0.00		Y	1,235.76	-		
		1	9998	0	Opening Balance			1,235.76	0.00	T9		1,235.76	-		
					1235.76 from SR 52	03/01/2016						1,235.76			
2	SI	PP002				01/01/2016	O/Bal	13,209.34	0.00		N	0.00	-		
		2	9998	0	Opening Balance			13,209.34	0.00	T9		0.00	-		
3	SI	HK006				01/01/2016	O/Bal	342.98	0.00		Y	342.98	-		
		3	9998	0	Opening Balance			342.98	0.00	T9		342.98	-		
					342.98 from SR 53	05/01/2016						342.98			
4	SI	PP004				01/01/2016	O/Bal	190.87	0.00		N	0.00	-		
		4	9998	0	Opening Balance			190.87	0.00	T9		0.00	-		
5	PI	MCS003				01/01/2016	O/Bal	1,943.26	0.00		Y	1,943.26	-		
		5	9998	0	Opening Balance			1,943.26	0.00	T9		1,943.26	-		
					1943.26 from PP 55	04/01/2016	0012672					1,943.26			
6	PI	WWW002				01/01/2016	O/Bal	288.29	0.00		Y	288.29	-		
		6	9998	0	Opening Balance			288.29	0.00	T9		288.29	-		
					288.29 from PP 69	11/01/2016	0012674					288.29			
7	PI	GRT005				01/01/2016	O/Bal	4,277.50	0.00		N	3,000.00	-		
		7	9998	0	Opening Balance			4,277.50	0.00	T9		3,000.00	-		
					3000.00 from PP 70	14/01/2016	0012675					3,000.00			
8	PI	FLW002				01/01/2016	O/Bal	923.46	0.00		Y	923.46	-		
		8	9998	0	Opening Balance			923.46	0.00	T9		923.46	-		
					923.46 from PP 54	04/01/2016	0012671					923.46			
9	JD	0050				01/01/2016	O/Bal	4,586.00	0.00		Y	4,586.00	-		
		9	0050	0	Opening Balance			4,586.00	0.00	T9		4,586.00	-		

| Date: | 29/08/2016 | | | | | **Justin Timbercrafts** | | | | | | | | Page: | 2 |
| Time: | 21:01:38 | | | | | **Audit Trail (Detailed)** | | | | | | | | | |

No	Type	A/C	N/C	Dept	Details	Date	Ref	Net	Tax	T/C	Pd	Paid	V	B	Bank Rec. Date
10	JC	9998				01/01/2016	O/Bal	4,586.00	0.00		Y	4,586.00	-		
		10	9998	0	Opening Balance			4,586.00	0.00	T9		4,586.00	-		
11	JD	0030				01/01/2016	O/Bal	3,684.00	0.00		Y	3,684.00	-		
		11	0030	0	Opening Balance			3,684.00	0.00	T9		3,684.00	-		
12	JC	9998				01/01/2016	O/Bal	3,684.00	0.00		Y	3,684.00	-		
		12	9998	0	Opening Balance			3,684.00	0.00	T9		3,684.00	-		
13	JD	1200				01/01/2016	O/Bal	11,203.30	0.00		Y	11,203.30	-	31/01/2016	
		13	1200	0	Opening Balance			11,203.30	0.00	T9		11,203.30	-		
14	JC	9998				01/01/2016	O/Bal	11,203.30	0.00		Y	11,203.30	-		
		14	9998	0	Opening Balance			11,203.30	0.00	T9		11,203.30	-		
15	JD	1230				01/01/2016	O/Bal	150.00	0.00		Y	150.00	-	31/01/2016	
		15	1230	0	Opening Balance			150.00	0.00	T9		150.00	-		
16	JC	9998				01/01/2016	O/Bal	150.00	0.00		Y	150.00	-		
		16	9998	0	Opening Balance			150.00	0.00	T9		150.00	-		
17	JC	4000				01/01/2016	O/Bal	17,293.50	0.00		Y	17,293.50	-		
		17	4000	0	Opening Balance			17,293.50	0.00	T9		17,293.50	-		
18	JD	9998				01/01/2016	O/Bal	17,293.50	0.00		Y	17,293.50	-		
		18	9998	0	Opening Balance			17,293.50	0.00	T9		17,293.50	-		
19	JC	4001				01/01/2016	O/Bal	19,224.70	0.00		Y	19,224.70	-		
		19	4001	0	Opening Balance			19,224.70	0.00	T9		19,224.70	-		
20	JD	9998				01/01/2016	O/Bal	19,224.70	0.00		Y	19,224.70	-		
		20	9998	0	Opening Balance			19,224.70	0.00	T9		19,224.70	-		
21	JC	4002				01/01/2016	O/Bal	10,260.45	0.00		Y	10,260.45	-		
		21	4002	0	Opening Balance			10,260.45	0.00	T9		10,260.45	-		
22	JD	9998				01/01/2016	O/Bal	10,260.45	0.00		Y	10,260.45	-		
		22	9998	0	Opening Balance			10,260.45	0.00	T9		10,260.45	-		
23	JC	4003				01/01/2016	O/Bal	5,431.40	0.00		Y	5,431.40	-		
		23	4003	0	Opening Balance			5,431.40	0.00	T9		5,431.40	-		
24	JD	9998				01/01/2016	O/Bal	5,431.40	0.00		Y	5,431.40	-		

| Date: | 29/08/2016 | | | | | | | Justin Timbercrafts | | | | | | Page: | 3 |
| Time: | 21:01:38 | | | | | | | Audit Trail (Detailed) | | | | | | | |

No	Type	A/C	N/C	Dept	Details	Date	Ref	Net	Tax	T/C	Pd	Paid	V	B	Bank Rec. Date
		24	9998	0	Opening Balance			5,431.40	0.00	T9		5,431.40	-		
25	JC	3000				01/01/2016	O/Bal	20,000.00	0.00		Y	20,000.00	-		
		25	3000	0	Opening Balance			20,000.00	0.00	T9		20,000.00	-		
26	JD	9998				01/01/2016	O/Bal	20,000.00	0.00		Y	20,000.00	-		
		26	9998	0	Opening Balance			20,000.00	0.00	T9		20,000.00	-		
27	JD	7100				01/01/2016	O/Bal	2,400.00	0.00		Y	2,400.00	-		
		27	7100	0	Opening Balance			2,400.00	0.00	T9		2,400.00	-		
28	JC	9998				01/01/2016	O/Bal	2,400.00	0.00		Y	2,400.00	-		
		28	9998	0	Opening Balance			2,400.00	0.00	T9		2,400.00	-		
29	JD	7104				01/01/2016	O/Bal	720.00	0.00		Y	720.00	-		
		29	7104	0	Opening Balance			720.00	0.00	T9		720.00	-		
30	JC	9998				01/01/2016	O/Bal	720.00	0.00		Y	720.00	-		
		30	9998	0	Opening Balance			720.00	0.00	T9		720.00	-		
31	JD	6201				01/01/2016	O/Bal	1,420.00	0.00		Y	1,420.00	-		
		31	6201	0	Opening Balance			1,420.00	0.00	T9		1,420.00	-		
32	JC	9998				01/01/2016	O/Bal	1,420.00	0.00		Y	1,420.00	-		
		32	9998	0	Opening Balance			1,420.00	0.00	T9		1,420.00	-		
33	JD	5000				01/01/2016	O/Bal	28,344.80	0.00		Y	28,344.80	-		
		33	5000	0	Opening Balance			28,344.80	0.00	T9		28,344.80	-		
34	JC	9998				01/01/2016	O/Bal	28,344.80	0.00		Y	28,344.80	-		
		34	9998	0	Opening Balance			28,344.80	0.00	T9		28,344.80	-		
35	JD	7504				01/01/2016	O/Bal	2,350.00	0.00		Y	2,350.00	-		
		35	7504	0	Opening Balance			2,350.00	0.00	T9		2,350.00	-		
36	JC	9998				01/01/2016	O/Bal	2,350.00	0.00		Y	2,350.00	-		
		36	9998	0	Opening Balance			2,350.00	0.00	T9		2,350.00	-		
37	JD	7304				01/01/2016	O/Bal	9,805.51	0.00		Y	9,805.51	-		
		37	7304	0	Opening Balance			9,805.51	0.00	T9		9,805.51	-		
38	JC	9998				01/01/2016	O/Bal	9,805.51	0.00		Y	9,805.51	-		
		38	9998	0	Opening Balance			9,805.51	0.00	T9		9,805.51	-		

| Date: | 29/08/2016 | | | | | | | Justin Timbercrafts | | | | | | Page: | 4 |
| Time: | 21:01:38 | | | | | | | Audit Trail (Detailed) | | | | | | | |

No	Type	A/C	N/C	Dept	Details	Date	Ref	Net	Tax	T/C	Pd	Paid	V	B	Bank Rec. Date
39	JC	1200				01/01/2016	TRF01	1,000.00	0.00		Y	1,000.00	R		31/01/2016
		39	1200	0	Bank Transfer			1,000.00	0.00	T9		1,000.00	-		
40	JD	1210				01/01/2016	TRF01	1,000.00	0.00		Y	1,000.00	N		
		40	1210	0	Bank Transfer			1,000.00	0.00	T9		1,000.00	-		
41	SI	HK006				02/01/2016	00300	146.00	29.20		Y	175.20	-		
		41	4001	0	Farm Collection x 8			56.00	11.20	T1		67.20	N		
					16.80 from SC 48	02/01/2016	55					16.80			
					50.40 from SR 68	11/01/2016	BACS					50.40			
		42	4000	0	Jungle Collection x 10			90.00	18.00	T1		108.00	N		
					108.00 from SR 68	11/01/2016	BACS					108.00			
43	SI	TW003				02/01/2016	00301	125.00	25.00		N	0.00	-		
		43	4001	0	Farm Collection x 5			35.00	7.00	T1		0.00	N		
		44	4000	0	Jungle Collection x 5			45.00	9.00	T1		0.00	N		
		45	4002	0	Pets Collection x 5			45.00	9.00	T1		0.00	N		
46	SI	HK006				04/01/2016	00302	100.00	20.00		N	0.00	-		
		46	4001	0	Farm Collection x 4			28.00	5.60	T1		0.00	N		
		47	4002	0	Pets Collection x 8			72.00	14.40	T1		0.00	N		
48	SC	HK006				02/01/2016	55	14.00	2.80		Y	16.80	-		
		48	4001	0	Farm collections			14.00	2.80	T1		16.80	N		
					16.80 to SI 41	02/01/2016	00300					16.80			
49	PI	DEC004				02/01/2016	2929/11	130.00	26.00		Y	156.00	-		
		49	6201	0	Advertising			130.00	26.00	T1		156.00	N		
					156.00 from PP 71	14/01/2016	0012676					156.00			
50	PI	GRT005				03/01/2016	GT2882	1,060.00	212.00		N	0.00	-		
		50	5000	0	Materials			1,060.00	212.00	T1		0.00	N		
51	PI	WWW002				06/01/2016	99128	240.00	48.00		N	0.00	-		
		51	5000	0	Materials			240.00	48.00	T1		0.00	N		
52	SR	TW003				03/01/2016		1,235.76	0.00		Y	1,235.76	R		31/01/2016
		52	1200	0	Sales Receipt			1,235.76	0.00	T9		1,235.76	-		
					1235.76 to SI 1	03/01/2016	O/Bal					1,235.76			
53	SR	HK006				05/01/2016		342.98	0.00		Y	342.98	R		31/01/2016

No	Type	A/C	N/C	Dept	Details	Date	Ref	Net	Tax	T/C	Pd	Paid	V	B	Bank Rec. Date
		53	1200	0	Sales Receipt			342.98	0.00	T9		342.98	-		
					342.98 to SI 3	05/01/2016	O/Bal					342.98			
54	PP	FLW002				04/01/2016	0012671	923.46	0.00		Y	923.46		R	31/01/2016
		54	1200	0	Purchase Payment			923.46	0.00	T9		923.46	-		
					923.46 to PI 8	04/01/2016	O/Bal					923.46			
55	PP	MCS003				04/01/2016	0012672	1,943.26	0.00		Y	1,943.26		R	31/01/2016
		55	1200	0	Purchase Payment			1,943.26	0.00	T9		1,943.26	-		
					1943.26 to PI 5	04/01/2016	O/Bal					1,943.26			
56	SC	PP004				05/01/2016	Bad Debt	190.87	0.00		N	0.00	-		
		56	8100	0	Bad Debt			190.87	0.00	T9		0.00	-		
57	CP	1230				05/01/2016	10	20.00	0.00		Y	20.00	-		
		57	7801	0	Window Cleaner			20.00	0.00	T0		20.00	N		
58	CP	1230				05/01/2016	11	20.00	4.00		Y	24.00	-		
		58	7504	0	5 x Xalculators			20.00	4.00	T1		24.00	N		
59	BR	1200				02/01/2016	Cash Sales	65.20	13.04		Y	78.24		R	31/01/2016
		59	4003	0	Cash Sales			65.20	13.04	T1		78.24	N		
60	BR	1200				04/01/2016	Cash Sales	85.25	17.05		Y	102.30		R	31/01/2016
		60	4003	0	Cash Sales			85.25	17.05	T1		102.30	N		
61	JD	3260				25/01/2016	JNL01	200.00	0.00		Y	200.00	-		
		61	3260	0	Transfer of cash for			200.00	0.00	T9		200.00	-		
62	JC	1200				25/01/2016	JNL01	200.00	0.00		Y	200.00		R	31/01/2016
		62	1200	0	Transfer of cash for			200.00	0.00	T9		200.00	-		
63	SI	FS001				06/01/2016	00303	80.00	16.00		N	0.00	-		
		63	4001	0	Farm Collection x 5			35.00	7.00	T1		0.00	N		
		64	4002	0	Pets Collection x 5			45.00	9.00	T1		0.00	N		
65	SI	TW003				06/01/2016	00304	270.00	54.00		N	0.00	-		
		65	4002	0	Pets Collection x 30			270.00	54.00	T1		0.00	N		
66	PI	MCS003				08/01/2016	3178	1,400.00	280.00		N	0.00	-		
		66	5000	0	Materials			1,400.00	280.00	T1		0.00	N		
67	PI	GRT005				11/01/2016	GT2916	560.00	112.00		N	0.00	-		

No	Type	A/C	N/C	Dept	Details	Date	Ref	Net	Tax	T/C	Pd	Paid	V	B	Bank Rec. Date
		67	5000	0	Materials			560.00	112.00	T1		0.00	N		
68	SR	11K006				11/01/2016	BACS	158.40	0.00		Y	158.40		R	31/01/2016
		68	1200	0	Sales Receipt			158.40	0.00	T9		158.40	-		
					50.40 to SI 41	11/01/2016	00300					50.40			
					108.00 to SI 42	11/01/2016	00300					108.00			
69	PP	WWW002				11/01/2016	0012674	288.29	0.00		Y	288.29		N	
		69	1200	0	Purchase Payment			288.29	0.00	T9		288.29	-		
					288.29 to PI 6	11/01/2016	O/Bal					288.29			
70	PP	GRT005				14/01/2016	0012675	3,000.00	0.00		Y	3,000.00		R	31/01/2016
		70	1200	0	Purchase Payment			3,000.00	0.00	T9		3,000.00	-		
					3000.00 to PI 7	14/01/2016	O/Bal					3,000.00			
71	PP	DEC004				14/01/2016	0012676	156.00	0.00		Y	156.00		N	
		71	1200	0	Purchase Payment			156.00	0.00	T9		156.00	-		
					156.00 to PI 49	14/01/2016	2929/11					156.00			
72	CP	1230				12/01/2016	12	14.80	0.00		Y	14.80	-		
		72	7400	0	Train Fare			14.80	0.00	T9		14.80	-		
73	CP	1230				14/01/2016	13	8.50	1.70		Y	10.20	-		
		73	7504	0	Photocopy paper			8.50	1.70	T1		10.20	N		
74	JD	1200				14/01/2016	JNL02	10,000.00	0.00		Y	10,000.00		R	31/01/2016
		74	1200	0	Loan Received			10,000.00	0.00	T9		10,000.00	-		
75	JC	2300				14/01/2016	JNL02	10,000.00	0.00		Y	10,000.00	-		
		75	2300	0	Loan Received			10,000.00	0.00	T9		10,000.00	-		
77	BP	1200				18/01/2016	S/O	400.00	0.00		Y	400.00		R	31/01/2016
		77	7100	0	P Smith - Rent			400.00	0.00	T9		400.00	-		
78	BP	1200				28/01/2016	S/O	120.00	0.00		Y	120.00		R	31/01/2016
		78	7100	0	Domley Council -			120.00	0.00	T9		120.00	-		
79	JD	7104				20/01/2016	JNL03	150.00	0.00		Y	150.00	-		
		79	7104	0	Correction of error			150.00	0.00	T9		150.00	-		
80	JC	7201				20/01/2016	JNL03	150.00	0.00		Y	150.00	-		
		80	7201	0	Correction of error			150.00	0.00	T9		150.00	-		

No	Type	A/C	N/C	Dept	Details	Date	Ref	Net	Tax	T/C	Pd	Paid	V	B	Bank Rec. Date
81	JC	1200				31/01/2016	TRF02	94.00	0.00		Y	94.00		R	31/01/2016
		81	1200	0	Bank Transfer			94.00	0.00	T9		94.00	-		
82	JD	1230				31/01/2016	TRF02	94.00	0.00		Y	94.00		-	
		82	1230	0	Bank Transfer			94.00	0.00	T9		94.00	-		
83	BP	1200				09/01/2016	0012673	208.33	41.67		Y	250.00		R	31/01/2016
		83	0030	0	Office Printer			208.33	41.67	T1		250.00	N		
84	BP	1200				28/01/2016		32.00	0.00		Y	32.00		R	31/01/2016
		84	7901	0	Charges incurred			32.00	0.00	T2		32.00	N		

Date: 29/08/2016
Time: 21:01:38
Justin Timbercrafts
Audit Trail (Detailed)
Page: 7

Aged Payables Report

Date: 29/08/2016
Time: 21:10:10
Justin Timbercrafts
Aged Creditors Analysis (Summary)
Page: 1

Report Date: 31/01/2016
Include future transactions: No
Exclude Later Payments: No

Supplier From:
Supplier To: ZZZZZZZZ

** NOTE: All report values are shown in Base Currency, unless otherwise indicated **

A/C	Name	Credit Limit	Turnover	Balance	Future	Current	Period 1	Period 2	Period 3	Older
GRT005	Grange Toys Ltd.	£ 10,000.00	5,897.50	3,221.50	0.00	1,944.00	1,277.50	0.00	0.00	0.00
MCS003	Matchsticks Ltd.	£ 5,000.00	3,343.26	1,680.00	0.00	1,680.00	0.00	0.00	0.00	0.00
WWW002	Willow Works Ltd	£ 8,500.00	528.29	288.00	0.00	288.00	0.00	0.00	0.00	0.00
	Totals:		9,769.05	5,189.50	0.00	3,912.00	1,277.50	0.00	0.00	0.00

Aged Receivables Report

Date: 29/08/2016
Time: 21:11:32
Justin Timbercrafts
Aged Debtors Analysis (Summary)
Page: 1

Report Date: 31/01/2016
Include future transactions: No
Exclude later payments: No

Customer From:
Customer To: ZZZZZZZZ

** NOTE: All report values are shown in Base Currency, unless otherwise indicated **

A/C	Name	Credit Limit	Turnover	Balance	Future	Current	Period 1	Period 2	Period 3	Older
FS001	Funnystuff Ltd	£ 1,000.00	80.00	96.00	0.00	96.00	0.00	0.00	0.00	0.00
HK006	Happykidz Ltd	£ 8,000.00	574.98	120.00	0.00	120.00	0.00	0.00	0.00	0.00
PP002	Perfect Pastimes Ltd	£ 15,000.00	13,209.34	13,209.34	0.00	0.00	13,209.34	0.00	0.00	0.00
PP004	Prettypops Ltd.	£ 5,000.00	0.00	0.00	0.00	-190.87	190.87	0.00	0.00	0.00
TW003	Toyways Plc	£ 5,000.00	1,630.76	474.00	0.00	474.00	0.00	0.00	0.00	0.00
	Totals:		15,495.08	13,899.34	0.00	499.13	13,400.21	0.00	0.00	0.00

Bank Current Account and Petty Cash Account

Date:	29/08/2016				Justin Timbercrafts					Page:	1
Time:	21:15:22				Nominal Activity						

Date From:	01/01/1980							N/C From:			
Date To:	29/08/2016							N/C To:	99999999		

Transaction From:	1
Transaction To:	99,999,999

N/C: 1200   Name: Bank Current Account   Account Balance: 14,713.97 DR

No	Type	Date	Account	Ref	Details	Dept	T/C	Value	Debit	Credit	V	B
13	JD	01/01/2016	1200	O/Bal	Opening Balance	0	T9	11,203.30	11,203.30			
39	JC	01/01/2016	1200	TRF01	Bank Transfer	0	T9	1,000.00		1,000.00		R
52	SR	03/01/2016	TW003		Sales Receipt	0	T9	1,235.76	1,235.76			R
53	SR	05/01/2016	HK006		Sales Receipt	0	T9	342.98	342.98			R
54	PP	04/01/2016	FLW002	0012671	Purchase Payment	0	T9	923.46		923.46		R
55	PP	04/01/2016	MCS003	0012672	Purchase Payment	0	T9	1,943.26		1,943.26		R
59	BR	02/01/2016	1200	Cash Sales	Cash Sales	0	T1	78.24	78.24		N	R
60	BR	04/01/2016	1200	Cash Sales	Cash Sales	0	T1	102.30	102.30		N	R
62	JC	25/01/2016	1200	JNL01	Transfer of cash for Justin's	0	T9	200.00		200.00		R
68	SR	11/01/2016	HK006	BACS	Sales Receipt	0	T9	158.40	158.40			R
69	PP	11/01/2016	WWW002	0012674	Purchase Payment	0	T9	288.29		288.29		N
70	PP	14/01/2016	GRT005	0012675	Purchase Payment	0	T9	3,000.00		3,000.00		R
71	PP	14/01/2016	DEC004	0012676	Purchase Payment	0	T9	156.00		156.00		N
74	JD	14/01/2016	1200	JNL02	Loan Received	0	T9	10,000.00	10,000.00			R
77	BP	18/01/2016	1200	S/O	P Smith - Rent	0	T9	400.00		400.00		R
78	BP	28/01/2016	1200	S/O	Dornley Council - Rates	0	T9	120.00		120.00		R
81	JC	31/01/2016	1200	TRF02	Bank Transfer	0	T9	94.00		94.00		R
83	BP	09/01/2016	1200	0012673	Office Printer	0	T1	250.00		250.00	N	R
84	BP	28/01/2016	1200		Charges incurred	0	T2	32.00		32.00	N	R
							Totals:		23,120.98	8,407.01		
							History Balance:		14,713.97			

N/C: 1230   Name: Petty Cash   Account Balance: 150.00 DR

No	Type	Date	Account	Ref	Details	Dept	T/C	Value	Debit	Credit	V	B
15	JD	01/01/2016	1230	O/Bal	Opening Balance	0	T9	150.00	150.00			
57	CP	05/01/2016	1230	10	Window Cleaner	0	T0	20.00		20.00	N	
58	CP	05/01/2016	1230	11	5 x Xalculators	0	T1	24.00		24.00	N	
72	CP	12/01/2016	1230	12	Train Fare	0	T9	14.80		14.80		
73	CP	14/01/2016	1230	13	Photocopy paper	0	T1	10.20		10.20	N	
76	CP	14/08/2016	1230	1289	Picture for Office Wall	0	T1	25.00		25.00	N	
82	JD	31/01/2016	1230	TRF02	Bank Transfer	0	T9	94.00	94.00			
							Totals:		244.00	94.00		
							History Balance:		150.00			

Journal Day Book

Date:	29/08/2016				Justin Timbercrafts			Page:	1
Time:	21:16:38				Day Books: Nominal Ledger				

Date From:	01/01/1980		N/C From:	
Date To:	31/12/2019		N/C To:	999999999

Transaction From:	1		Dept From:	0
Transaction To:	99,999,999		Dept To:	999

No	Type	N/C	Date	Ref	Ex.Ref	Details	Dept	T/C	Debit	Credit	V	B
9	JD	0050	01/01/2016	O/Bal		Opening Balance	0	T9	4,586.00		-	-
10	JC	9998	01/01/2016	O/Bal		Opening Balance	0	T9		4,586.00	-	-
11	JD	0030	01/01/2016	O/Bal		Opening Balance	0	T9	3,684.00		-	-
12	JC	9998	01/01/2016	O/Bal		Opening Balance	0	T9		3,684.00	-	-
13	JD	1200	01/01/2016	O/Bal		Opening Balance	0	T9	11,203.30		-	-
14	JC	9998	01/01/2016	O/Bal		Opening Balance	0	T9		11,203.30	-	-
15	JD	1230	01/01/2016	O/Bal		Opening Balance	0	T9	150.00		-	-
16	JC	9998	01/01/2016	O/Bal		Opening Balance	0	T9		150.00	-	-
17	JC	4000	01/01/2016	O/Bal		Opening Balance	0	T9		17,293.50	-	-
18	JD	9998	01/01/2016	O/Bal		Opening Balance	0	T9	17,293.50		-	-
19	JC	4001	01/01/2016	O/Bal		Opening Balance	0	T9		19,224.70	-	-
20	JD	9998	01/01/2016	O/Bal		Opening Balance	0	T9	19,224.70		-	-
21	JC	4002	01/01/2016	O/Bal		Opening Balance	0	T9		10,260.45	-	-
22	JD	9998	01/01/2016	O/Bal		Opening Balance	0	T9	10,260.45		-	-
23	JC	4003	01/01/2016	O/Bal		Opening Balance	0	T9		5,431.40	-	-
24	JD	9998	01/01/2016	O/Bal		Opening Balance	0	T9	5,431.40		-	-
25	JC	3000	01/01/2016	O/Bal		Opening Balance	0	T9		20,000.00	-	-
26	JD	9998	01/01/2016	O/Bal		Opening Balance	0	T9	20,000.00		-	-
27	JD	7100	01/01/2016	O/Bal		Opening Balance	0	T9	2,400.00		-	-
28	JC	9998	01/01/2016	O/Bal		Opening Balance	0	T9		2,400.00	-	-
29	JD	7104	01/01/2016	O/Bal		Opening Balance	0	T9	720.00		-	-
30	JC	9998	01/01/2016	O/Bal		Opening Balance	0	T9		720.00	-	-
31	JD	6201	01/01/2016	O/Bal		Opening Balance	0	T9	1,420.00		-	-
32	JC	9998	01/01/2016	O/Bal		Opening Balance	0	T9		1,420.00	-	-
33	JD	5000	01/01/2016	O/Bal		Opening Balance	0	T9	28,344.80		-	-
34	JC	9998	01/01/2016	O/Bal		Opening Balance	0	T9		28,344.80	-	-
35	JD	7504	01/01/2016	O/Bal		Opening Balance	0	T9	2,350.00		-	-
36	JC	9998	01/01/2016	O/Bal		Opening Balance	0	T9		2,350.00	-	-
37	JD	7304	01/01/2016	O/Bal		Opening Balance	0	T9	9,805.51		-	-
38	JC	9998	01/01/2016	O/Bal		Opening Balance	0	T9		9,805.51	-	-
39	JC	1200	01/01/2016	TRF01		Bank Transfer	0	T9		1,000.00	-	R
40	JD	1210	01/01/2016	TRF01		Bank Transfer	0	T9	1,000.00		-	N
61	JD	3260	25/01/2016	JNL01		Transfer of cash for Justin's	0	T9	200.00		-	-
62	JC	1200	25/01/2016	JNL01		Transfer of cash for Justin's	0	T9		200.00	-	R
74	JD	1200	14/01/2016	JNL02		Loan Received	0	T9	10,000.00		-	R
75	JC	2300	14/01/2016	JNL02		Loan Received	0	T9		10,000.00	-	-
79	JD	7104	20/01/2016	JNL03		Correction of error recording	0	T9	150.00		-	-
80	JC	7201	20/01/2016	JNL03		Correction of error recording	0	T9		150.00	-	-
81	JC	1200	31/01/2016	TRF02		Bank Transfer	0	T9		94.00	-	R
82	JD	1230	31/01/2016	TRF02		Bank Transfer	0	T9	94.00		-	-
								Totals:	148,317.66	148,317.66		

Bank Statement

Date:	29/08/2016					Page:	1

Bank Statement

1200
Bank Current Account
Currency: Pound Sterling

Justin Timbercrafts
27 West Lane
Domley
DN22 4RD

Bank Balance: 14713.97

Date From: 01/01/1980
Date To: 29/08/2016

No	Date	Ref	Details	Payments	Receipts	Balance
			B/Fwd Balance			11,203.30
39	01/01/2016	TRF01	Bank Transfer	1,000.00		10,203.30
52	03/01/2016		Sales Receipt		1,235.76	11,439.06
53	05/01/2016		Sales Receipt		342.98	11,782.04
54	04/01/2016	0012671	Purchase Payment	923.46		10,858.58
55	04/01/2016	0012672	Purchase Payment	1,943.26		8,915.32
59	02/01/2016	Cash Sales	Cash Sales		78.24	8,993.56
60	04/01/2016	Cash Sales	Cash Sales		102.30	9,095.86
62	25/01/2016	JNL01	Transfer of cash for Justin's	200.00		8,895.86
68	11/01/2016	BACS	Sales Receipt		158.40	9,054.26
70	14/01/2016	0012675	Purchase Payment	3,000.00		6,054.26
74	14/01/2016	JNL02	Loan Received		10,000.00	16,054.26
77	18/01/2016	S/O	P Smith - Rent	400.00		15,654.26
78	28/01/2016	S/O	Domley Council - Rates	120.00		15,534.26
81	31/01/2016	TRF02	Bank Transfer	94.00		15,440.26
83	09/01/2016	0012673	Office Printer	250.00		15,190.26
84	28/01/2016		Charges incurred	32.00		15,158.26

INDEX